D1765537

4.7.2017

for

tl   a

mella

h Lee

FP

Day

FP
02/15

CAMBRIDGE
UNIVERSITY PRESS

CAMBRIDGE
UNIVERSITY PRESS

University Printing House, Cambridge CB2 8BS, United Kingdom

Cambridge University Press is part of the University of Cambridge.

It furthers the University's mission by disseminating knowledge in the pursuit of education, learning and research at the highest international levels of excellence.

www.cambridge.org
Information on this title: www.cambridge.org/9780521724579

© Cambridge University Press 2008

First published 2008
8th printing 2014

Printed in Dubai by Oriental Press

A catalogue record for this publication is available from the British Library

ISBN 9780521724579 Cambridge English for the Media Student's Book with Audio CD
ISBN 9780511401022 Online resources

Introduction

The main aims of *Cambridge English for the Media* are to improve your communication skills at work and your English language knowledge in key areas of the media. To give you as much practice as possible, each of the eight units contains:

- discussion of the media topic
- listening activities reflecting everyday media scenarios which allow you to learn the language used in different working situations, for example meetings, dealing with clients, and giving feedback
- realistic speaking activities that give you plenty of practice of the language you've looked at
- reading and writing practice, based on authentic media documents
- engaging topics and articles which ensure that learning is interesting and motivating

On the audio you hear people in the kind of media situations that you can encounter as a media professional, for example taking part in an editorial meeting, giving a briefing over the phone, shooting on location, giving a pitch, designing a home page, presenting an advertisement to a client and analysing feedback.

How to use *Cambridge English for the Media* for self-study

If you are working on your own, you can do the units in any order you like. Choose the topic that you want to look at and work through the unit doing the exercises and checking your answers in the answer key. Note down any mistakes you make, and go back and listen or read again to see what the problem was. It's a good idea to listen to the audio more than once and to read the audioscript afterwards to check that you've understood. For the speaking activities, *think* about what you would say in the situation. You could also try talking about the discussion points with your colleagues. Audioscripts and a complete answer key for the exercises are at the back of the book.

We hope you enjoy using the course. If you have any comments on *Cambridge English for Media*, we'd love to hear them. You can email us at englishforthemedia@cambridge.org

Elizabeth

Nick

Nick Ceramella has a degree in modern foreign languages and literatures and teaching qualifications in both English language and literature. He is also a qualified secondary school teacher trainer. He has been a teacher for over thirty years, with extensive experience gained through his work in various Italian universities as well as in Britain, Brazil, Russia and Montenegro. He currently teaches English for media studies and business communication in the Department of Media Studies at the Libera Università Maria Santissima Assunta, Rome, as well as English and American literatures at the University for Foreigners, Perugia.

Elizabeth Lee has a degree in French and a masters in English Literature, as well as certificate and diploma qualifications in TEFL. She is a lecturer at the Università di Roma. She has been teaching for over 12 years and is an experienced author, having worked on ELT material for secondary school learners. She is also an experienced teacher trainer.

UNIT 1 Newspapers

- Writing headlines
- Analysing newspaper articles
- Practising interview skills
- Planning and writing a newspaper article

Writing headlines

1 a In pairs, discuss the following questions.

1 Which newspapers do you read? Why?
2 What's the biggest news story in your country at the moment?
3 Why are headlines important?
4 Do you find it difficult to read headlines in English? Explain why / why not.

b Understanding headlines in a foreign language can be difficult. Look at the headlines in Exercise 1c (1–8) and decide what you think each story is about.

c Now match the headlines (1–8) to their everyday English equivalents (a–h).

1 **Paris probe proves palace innocent**

2 **Love's Labour's Lost**

3 **Choose That Girl! Madge jets to Africa to adopt girl**

4 **US cool on climate change**

5 **Weeping mum damns teenage killer thug**

6 **Family's pet dog butchered**

7 **Comedian rapped over slang word by TV watchdog**

8 **Government to axe 3,500 post offices**

a The government is going to close 3,500 post offices.

b The US government is not keen on a new environmental policy.

c A family dog has been brutally killed.

d An investigation into Princess Diana's death shows the British royal family were not involved.

e Labour's Prime Minister and Chancellor of the Exchequer do not agree on government policies.

f A popular comedian, who pretends to be a rapper, is in trouble with the Independent Television Commission for using offensive words on TV.

g The singer Madonna has flown to Africa to adopt a child.

h A mother refuses to forgive the people who killed her daughter.

d Look at the headlines in Exercise 1c again. Decide which of the following questions can easily be answered by reading them.

- What happened?
- Where did it happen?
- When did it happen?
- Who did what?
- Why did it happen?

e In pairs, discuss the following questions.

1 Which of the headlines got your interest? Why?
2 Which headlines would you put on the front page of a newspaper? Explain your choice(s).
3 If you were the editor of a popular daily, which would be your lead story (the most important story of the day)? Explain your choice.
4 How do you think the stories continue?

f Look at the headlines in Exercise 1c again and answer the following questions.

1 Which of the following kinds of word are omitted from the headlines?
articles, auxiliary verbs, main verbs, nouns, pronouns
2 Which of the following verb forms are used?
to + infinitive, present simple, past simple, past participle
3 Which of the following are used?
abbreviations, commas, full stops, exclamation marks

2 a Look at the following sentences which have been turned into headlines. Make a list of what changes have been made to turn them into headlines.

1 Three people have been killed in a terrible shop fire.

> **Terrible shop fire kills 3**

Articles, preposition and one noun have been omitted; passive to active; present perfect to present simple; word to numeral (three/3)

2 The Boston Red Sox have humiliated the Toronto Blue Jays, who lost 8–0.

> **Boston Red Sox humiliate Toronto Blue Jays 8–0**

3 Police mistakes have led to 183 crimes not being detected.

> **Police mistakes: 183 crimes not detected**

4 A judge has sentenced a lottery winner to jail for a bank robbery.

> **Lottery winner jailed for robbery**

b In pairs, look at the following sentences and turn them into headlines.

1 A very rare breed of bird has returned to the United Kingdom after more than 400 years.
2 A drunk driver caused an accident on route 95, which resulted in two people being killed.
3 The Australian Prime Minister is going to open a new hospital in Melbourne.

3 **a** Newspapers use several language devices in order to create eye-catching headlines. Complete the following table using more examples from the headlines in Exercise 1c. Some headlines may go in more than one column.

Language device	Example	More examples
Play on words words with more than one meaning	US <u>cool</u> on climate change (cool = not warm; to be cool on = to not be keen on)	Comedian <u>rapped</u> over slang word by TV watchdog (to rap sb = to criticise sb formally; to rap = to perform rap)
Cultural references	Love's Labour's Lost (the name of a play by Shakespeare)	
Alliteration the use of the same sound or sounds, especially consonants, at the beginning of several words that are close together	<u>P</u>aris <u>p</u>robe <u>p</u>roves <u>p</u>alace innocent	
Emphatic language words which have a stronger effect	<u>Weeping</u> mum <u>damns</u> teenage killer thug	

b In pairs, make a list of any English-language tabloid and broadsheet newspapers you know.

c The tabloid press sometimes uses words that are not common in everyday English. This is known as *tabloidese*. Match each of the <u>underlined</u> *tabloidese* words in the sentences (1–5) to their meanings (a–e).

1	Guilty pupil <u>vows</u> to return stolen exam papers	a	a mistake
2	Husband and wife <u>row</u> keeps neighbours awake	b	anger
3	Government <u>blunder</u>: 1 million taxpayers' personal details lost	c	to promise
4	Voters' <u>fury</u> at election results	d	to question
5	Police <u>quiz</u> man over Greenwood Bank robbery	e	an argument

d In pairs, discuss which language devices have been used in the following headlines and what each story might be about.

1 **Titanic disaster: new cruise ship has no customers**

2 **European Union: to be or not to be?**

3 **Gorgeous George – Clooney conquers Cannes**

4 **Bomb carnage kills 1 and injures 26**

5 **Space reality show axed**

e In groups, role play an editorial meeting for a national daily newspaper. Discuss and then decide on the following questions.
- What type of newspaper is it: tabloid or broadsheet?
- What are the most important stories of the day (use your answers to Exercise 1a, question 2)?
- What are the headlines going to be for those stories?
- Which headlines will you put on the front page?
- Which will be your lead story?

Analysing newspaper articles

4 a In groups, discuss the following questions.

1 How objective are newspapers in your country?
2 What do you know about the political slant of newspapers in English-speaking countries?
3 Do you think newspapers should be objective? Explain why / why not.
4 Which kind of article do you prefer: opinion-based or fact-based?

b In 2005, a shopping centre in Britain decided to ban people from wearing hooded tops (hoodies). In groups, discuss the following questions.

1 What do you think was the reason for banning hooded tops?
2 How do you think this might have been reported in the press?

c Read the following two headlines from the British national press. In pairs, decide which of the following adjectives best describe the slant each of the articles will have.

| liberal | emotive | conservative | reactionary | neutral |

1

Reclaim our streets: hoodies and baddies

2

Under that hoodie is a child like yours

d Choice of vocabulary can affect the slant of a newspaper article. Look at the following vocabulary items from the two articles. In pairs, decide which words are more emotive and which are more neutral.

muggers	ban	intimidated
low-level disorder	discrimination	yobs
law-abiding	teenagers	shoplifting
fed up with	crime epidemic	weapon
terrorise	outsider	

e Read the two articles on page 10. Match the headlines to the articles. Were your predictions in Exercise 4c correct?

f Read the first paragraph of the articles again. How do they differ in the way they engage the reader's attention?

A

1 THEY are the uniform of thugs and muggers and the sight of young people wearing them makes law-abiding citizens feel scared.

5 Hooded tops and baseball caps have been adopted by cowardly yobs up and down the land to hide their faces from CCTV cameras while they commit crime 10 or terrorise victims unable to identify them.

So the decision by Bluewater shopping centre in Kent to ban the clothing has pleased people fed 15 up with constant intimidation.

The Prime Minister backed the decision. He said: "I agree with it."

The Bluewater ban will be met by cries of discrimination from 20 innocent teenagers who argue they should be allowed to wear what they want.

But police say that more than half of robberies in some parts are 25 carried out by thugs in hoods and baseball caps – a gangster-style look made popular by US rap stars such as Eminem.

The ban is no different to stopping 30 people wearing crash helmets in banks in an effort to prevent armed robberies. It may also help to stop Britain's retail crime epidemic, which is said to cost 35 the industry £2 billion a year. A similar scheme in Basildon, Essex, led to a decrease in shoplifting.

B

1 Does Prince William own a hoodie? Do the Prime Minister's children have these clothes in their wardrobes? I imagine they do because for teenagers they are almost a uniform.

5 Some hoodies may even have been bought at the Bluewater shopping centre in Kent, which banned the wearing of hoods and baseball caps in its centre.

The Prime Minister approves of the ban as he has realised that many voters feel anxiety about 10 yobbishness and "low-level disorder".

Many people feel intimidated and threatened by gangs of kids on their bikes with their hoods up. Kids hanging around on street corners, in front of cafes, in parks... Often they do no harm, but they don't 15 move out of the way for old ladies, for women with pushchairs, for anyone. They behave as if they own the streets and most of the time most of us let them.

Yet to blame all this on clothes is too simplistic. To confuse anti-social behaviour with a clothes 20 item worn by everyone from Coldplay singer Chris Martin to the middle-aged man going to the gym is a mistake.

It is true that hoods and caps provide anonymity for those up to no good. They cover faces and make it 25 impossible for victims to recognise their attackers. What's more, they are the prime weapon against what we are told will ultimately protect us: CCTV. They record crimes as they are happening, but do nothing to prevent them happening. In such an 30 environment there is a feeling that the streets and town centres do not properly belong to us and the hoodie has become a symbol for those we fear have taken control.

The challenge is to make these hooded kids feel part 35 of something. The youth with his hood up is in his own little world: he becomes an outsider.

The moment he takes it down he may look surprisingly like one of your own children.

g In pairs, look at the following statement and discuss whether you agree with it. Explain why / why not.

"All words have bias. No choice is impartial."

h Look at the articles and headlines again. Make a list of the words the journalists use to refer to (1) young people and (2) crime. In pairs, discuss what effect this creates.

i Read the articles again and decide if the following statements are True (T) or False (F).

1 All teenagers wear hoodies.
2 Prince William has definitely got a hoodie.
3 The Prime Minister thinks that banning hoodies is a good idea.
4 In some areas of the country more than 50% of robberies are committed by people wearing hoodies and baseball caps.
5 According to the writer of the second article, most people let gangs of kids do as they want.
6 Both articles see a connection between young people feeling alienated from society and the wearing of hoods.

j In pairs, discuss the following questions.

1 Does your country have similar problems with young people?
2 Which article do you agree with the most? Explain your choice.
3 What effect do you think each article will have on its reader?

5 **a** Match the cohesion techniques (1–4) to the examples from the articles (a–d).

1	use of personal pronouns	a	It is true that hoods and caps provide anonymity for those up to no good.
2	word groups / synonyms	b	Some hoodies may even have been bought at the Bluewater shopping centre in Kent, which banned the wearing of hoods and baseball caps in its centre.
3	use of linking words		
4	omission of words that can be understood from the previous text or context	c	The Prime Minister backed the decision. He said: "I agree with it."
		d	Yet to blame all this on clothes is too simplistic.

b In pairs, find more examples of each technique in the articles.

c Underline the pronouns in the following extract from the second article. Then say what or who they refer to.

They record crimes – 'they' refers to
　　　　　　　CCTV cameras

> They record crimes as they are happening, but do nothing to prevent them happening. In such an environment there is a feeling that the streets and town centres do not properly belong to us and the hoodie has become a symbol for those we fear have taken control.

d Look at the underlined words in the extracts below and then answer the following questions.

- The Bluewater ban will be met by cries of discrimination …
  (Text A lines 18–19)
- … Britain's retail crime epidemic, which is said to cost the industry £2 billion a year. (Text A lines 33–35)

1 Are the underlined structures active or passive?
2 Why is this structure used in each sentence?
　a To avoid mentioning who does the action.
　b To create cohesion: the subject of the sentence is the same as the topic of previous sentences.

e In pairs, make a list of other passive structures in the articles. Then decide why the passive is being used.

f Now write a short article about anti-social behaviour or another issue in your country. Remember to use the techniques from this unit, including the passive, to make your article more cohesive.

Practising interview skills

6 a **In pairs, discuss the following questions.**

1 Do you ever interview people for work? Who? Why?
2 If you could interview any person in the world, who would you choose? Explain why. What would you ask them?
3 What makes a good interview?

b ▶1.1 **Katie Jones, a journalist, is being interviewed about her career in the media world for a newspaper article. Listen to the first part of the interview and tick (✓) the topics she talks about.**

☐ Her family and friends   ☐ Her past jobs and education
☐ Television and the Internet   ☐ Her present job

c ▶1.2 **Now listen to the second part of the interview and decide if the following statements are True (T) or False (F).**

1 Katie thinks that newspaper format has changed during her career.
2 Newspaper sales are not increasing.
3 More and more people like to watch news on the Internet.
4 Journalists are becoming less important.

d ▶1.1/1.2 **Look at the plan Simon Young made for the article he is going to write about Katie Jones. Listen to both parts of the interview again and fill in the missing information.**

PROFILE: KATIE JONES

Training
Cardiff: postgraduate course in journalism - 1 year

Jobs
Southsea Times: (1) __trainee_____ - 12 months
Hatherfield Herald: (2) _____ then
(3) sub-_____ - 12 months
Southern Mail: district news reporter, (4) _____ ,
correspondent, assistant news editor, (5) _____ news editor
UK Radio Wales: producer of The (6) _____ Show
Bristol Council: (7) head of _____ office

Opinion on current UK newspaper market
Tough: most newspapers' (8) _____ is not rising
Newspapers are (9) _____ - e.g. reporters trained to use
(10) _____

Future of print newspapers
Might not survive (11) _____ age

Media inspiration
Henry Linton, veteran (12) _____ correspondent for UK Radio

e In pairs, discuss the following questions.

1 Do you agree with Katie Jones' predictions about the future of newspapers? Explain why / why not.
2 What changes have you seen in newspapers in recent years?
3 Is there anyone in the media world who you admire?

f Look at the following jumbled sentences from the interview. Put the words in the correct order to form the questions that the journalist asked Katie Jones.

1 last / how long / the postgraduate course / did ?
   How long did the postgraduate course last?
2 enjoy / the positions / did you ?
3 as head of the press office / continue / will you ?
4 a new position / looking for / are you ?
5 newspapers / during your career / changed / have ?
6 would you / the present newspaper market / how / in the UK / describe ?
7 coming to an end / is / the era of print newspapers ?
8 is / your media inspiration / who ?
9 for people ... / any advice / have / Do you ?

g Complete the following table using questions 1–9 in Exercise 6f.

a Question word	b Auxiliary verb	c Subject	d Main verb	e Rest of question
1 How long	did	the postgraduate course	last?	–
2 –	Did	you	enjoy	the positions?
3				
4				
5				
6				
7				
8				
9				

h The phrases below are taken from the interview. Complete the following table by writing the phrases (1–8) in the correct column.

1 Pleased to meet you.
2 What exactly were they?
3 Right ...
4 Sorry to interrupt, but ...
5 Could you be more specific?
6 OK ...
7 Sorry to butt in (again) ...
8 Why do you say that?

Introductions	Interrupting	Hesitating	Asking for detail
How do you do?	Hold on, ...	Well ...	What exactly do you mean?
Nice to meet you.	Could I just say something?	You know ...	
I'm ...	Sorry, but ...	I mean ...	
	Can I interrupt for a moment?	So ...	
	Hang on a minute, ...		

i Student A, close your book and see how many phrases you can remember. Student B, correct Student A's mistakes. Swap roles and practise again.

j In pairs, plan and role play an interview. First, write (at least) five facts about your job your partner can ask you about. If you haven't started work yet, include facts about your future career plans. Exchange your facts with your partner. Interview your partner for a newspaper article about their life. Use their facts and ask questions to find out more details. Use the following question words and phrases in the box in Exercise 6h to help you. Swap roles and practise again.

Planning and writing a newspaper article

7 a Look at the following statements about news writing. Number the statements from 1 to 5: 1 = strongly agree, 5 = strongly disagree.

- ☐ Journalism, in the Anglo-Saxon tradition, is informal rather than formal.
- ☐ The most important things in a good news story are shock, surprise and contrast.
- ☐ A good journalist can always write a short story, even if they would prefer to write a longer version.
- ☐ If you can't get the reader's attention in the first sentence, they won't bother to read the rest of the story.
- ☐ It's house style, not good journalism, that makes a newspaper successful.

b In groups, discuss your answers to Exercise 7a.

8 a In pairs, look at the following definition of house style and then make a list of other possible house style features.

punctuation, spelling ...

> **house style** *(noun)*
> the preferred style of spelling, punctuation, etc. used in a publishing house or by a specific publication.

b If you have access to the Internet, visit these websites and check and compare your lists.

www.guardian.co.uk/styleguide
www.economist.com/research/styleguide

c In pairs, look at the following reasons why house style is important. Decide which are true and explain why.

1 Helps maintain consistency
2 Shows how stylish the newspaper is
3 Creates a brand image

d Complete the following table using the correct house style features in Article B (from the *Daily Mail*) on page 10.

House style feature	*Daily Mail* house style	Alternative house style
Punctuation	" "	' '
Spelling		realized
Capitalisation		prime minister
Foreign words		café
Use of American/British/Australian English		shopping mall

9 a Have you ever written a newspaper article? If so, what steps did you follow? Look at the steps for writing a newspaper article below and put them into a logical order.

- ☐ Check your article for mistakes
- ☐ Plan (organise and paragraph your ideas)
- ☐ Brainstorm the topic (write down ideas connected to the article)
- ☐ Research the story
- ☐ Write the introduction
- ☐ Conclude
- ☐ Write the main body of the article

b Read the following ideas that a journalist brainstormed for an article. Then write a sentence summarising what you think the newspaper article will be about.

Where? private kindergarten in Ipswich, Suffolk

When? 11–12 pm?

How? broke wall with tools

Victims? a nursery school: "We were so shocked we were targeted when we are just a nursery."

What taken? a safe

Police: "We are doing all we can to arrest the thief."

c Look at the headline and photo from the article. Do they give you any extra information about the story?

Gang breaks into kindergarten through hole in the wall

d Read the main body of the article that has been written based on the notes in Exercise 9b. Is the summary you wrote in Exercise 9b correct?

...

Manager Jacqui Mayes, 27, said: "We were so shocked we were targeted when we are just a nursery. They caused so much damage to get in. It seemed premeditated. It looks like they had the right equipment for the job."

Ms Mayes said her 20 staff at the kindergarten, which is attended by 130 young children, were baffled by the highly professional raid. There's no way anyone could have known how much money was in there and the safe could not be seen through the window as the glass is tinted.

...

e In pairs, look at the following possible introductions to the article (1–3). Choose the best one and discuss what is wrong with the others.

1

Thieves broke into a nursery school yesterday and took whatever they could. According to a witness they must have used a wheelbarrow to move the loot. The criminals have vanished into thin air.

2

A burglary took place in Ipswich sometime yesterday. The thieves made a big hole in a wall when they entered. It seems a certain amount of money was found and stolen. Police say they do not have any clues but they know these kinds of burglaries are quite common in the county.

3

Staff at Ipswich private Kindergarten in Suffolk were shocked after thieves smashed a wall exactly where the safe was. The heavy cashbox containing about £1,200 was taken away in the nursery's wheelie bin.

f Now look at the following possible conclusions to the article (1–3). Choose the best one and discuss what is wrong with the others.

1

> The kindergarten joins the list of victims of crime in Britain. We hope the police catch the criminals soon.

2

> "One thing we have noticed is that our wheelie bin has been stolen," she said. "We believe they used a wheelbarrow to move the safe from the office to the wheelie bin and then used the wheelie bin to take it away. Police have been here and the scene has been fingerprinted. We can only hope someone is caught for the burglary." A police spokesperson said: "We are doing all we can to catch the culprit."

3

> The victims said they had noticed that their wheelie bin had been stolen and think it is connected to the burglary. The police have been to the kindergarten and are doing as much as possible to catch the thieves.

g Look at the following notes written by a journalist about the theft of a prize show cat. In pairs, write a short article for a newspaper. Use the techniques described in this unit to help you.

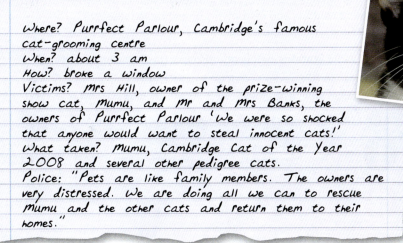

> Where? Purrfect Parlour, Cambridge's famous cat-grooming centre
> When? about 3 am
> How? broke a window
> Victims? Mrs Hill, owner of the prize-winning show cat, Mumu, and Mr and Mrs Banks, the owners of Purrfect Parlour 'We were so shocked that anyone would want to steal innocent cats!'
> What taken? Mumu, Cambridge Cat of the Year 2008 and several other pedigree cats.
> Police: "Pets are like family members. The owners are very distressed. We are doing all we can to rescue Mumu and the other cats and return them to their homes."

h Exchange your story with another pair. Read and make any corrections to their article and give it a headline.

i In groups, research a local news story. Make notes and write an article for an English-speaking newspaper.

UNIT 2 Radio

- Understanding the language of radio presenters
- Understanding the production process
- Planning a news list
- Giving post-production feedback

Understanding the language of radio presenters

1 **a** **In pairs, discuss the following questions.**

   1   Which do you prefer: TV or radio? Explain why.
   2   How often do you listen to the radio?
   3   To what extent is radio regulated or deregulated in your country? Are there a lot of government controls and restrictions on the radio industry?
   4   Which radio stations are the most popular in your country?

b **Look at the BBC radio stations below and discuss the following questions.**

   1   Do you ever listen to BBC radio? What do you listen to?
   2   Which station below would you most like to listen to? Explain why.

c **Match the BBC radio stations (1–6) to the genres (a–f).**

   1   **BBC RADIO 1** The best new music and entertainment

   2   **BBC RADIO 2** The most listened-to station in the UK

   3   **BBC RADIO 3** 90–93FM Classical, jazz and world music, drama and the arts

   4   **BBC RADIO 4** 92–95FM The home of intelligent speech radio

   5   **BBC RADIO 5 live** The home of live news and live sport

   6   **BBC Worldwide** Impartial news and reports from around the world

   a   Classical music

   b   Global news and documentary

   c   Popular music; youth-oriented

   d   News and sport

   e   Easy-listening music; adult-oriented

   f   News, current affairs and arts

d ▶2.1 **Listen to the following excerpts from different radio stations. Decide which genre of radio station they belong to. Use the genres a–f in Exercise 1c to help you.**

1 _Popular music or easy-listening music_   5 _____
2 _____   6 _____
3 _____   7 _____
4 _____   8 _____

e ▶2.1 **Listen again and tick (✓) the phrases that you hear.**

Introducing the show/presenter/DJ	Introducing guests/features/news	Introducing music
It's 6 o'clock on Monday 24th September. This is *The Morning Show* with John Gray in London …	In this programme, we'll be talking to the education minister about student debt.	Next up is *All Summer Long* by Kid Rock.
It's 8 o'clock, and you're having breakfast with me, Amanda Green.	Let's talk to Jonathon White, our football correspondent.	We've still got Madonna's *Ray Of Light* to play for you, and a track from The Beatles, but first, The Foo Fighters' *Learn To Fly*.
And now it's time for *Everyday Women* … with Carla Morris.	Still to come in the next half hour, we interview …	That was The Saturdays with *If This Is Love*. Before that you heard *Forever* from Chris Brown.
You're listening to UK Radio FM.	We'll be speaking to the Prime Minister at ten past eight.	Here's the second movement of Beethoven's *Emperor Concerto*, performed by the Berlin Philharmonic Orchestra and conducted by Heinrich Erhard.
I'm Gemma Wilson and welcome to *In Focus*.	… but now over to the newsroom.	
I'm Mo Ace and this is a free podcast.	This week, Rahim Anwar presents a programme about the poet Auden …	This is the brilliant Nick Cave with *Into My Arms*.
	Coming up, the news, with …	

f **Correct the mistakes in the following extracts from radio broadcasts.**

1 You're listening at Radio Australia. I'm Gil Brennen and welcome at *Good Morning Australia*.
2 Here's Bach's Concerto for keyboard in D major, performed with Alison Balsom and Colm Carey.
3 It's Tuesday the 19th January. This is *Report*, with Bill Noles and Justine Welsh. Still to come in the next half hour, we'll be interviewing to Janie Kirk.
4 That was Coldplay by *Viva la vida*. Before that, you heard *Rockstar* of Nickelback.
5 This week, John Walsh presents a programme with finding work on the Internet.

g ▶2.2 **Listen to the extracts and check your answers.**

h Imagine you had a 15-minute slot on a national radio station. What genre would it be? What music would you include? How would you introduce it? Write the script for your slot.

i Now either record your broadcast and play it back to your class, or read your broadcast 'live' to your class. As you listen to the different broadcasts, decide who you think would make the best DJ / radio presenter.

2 **a** **In pairs, discuss the following questions.**

1 Would you like to work in radio? Explain why / why not.
2 Do you know anyone who works in radio? If so, how did he/she find the job?

b **Read the radio commissioning brief and answer the following questions.**

1 What is a radio commissioning brief?
2 Who do you think wrote this brief?
3 Who is it written for?
4 Where would you expect to see this type of document?

London 1 documentaries

London 1

Listeners

London 1 is the voice of young London and serves a **key audience**: the under-25s.

Music is at the heart of the station, which is the most listened-to youth station in London, with an audience of nearly 60% of London's 15–24s.

Documentaries

When it comes to documentaries, the audience is interested in the world around them, but does not want to be lectured or told what to think. The tone and approach must always be peer-to-peer rather than parental. London 1 will continue to commission documentaries to entertain and engage, but the audio is only part of what we are commissioning. Producers will be expected to provide, in addition to the broadcast programme:

- Selected highlights to be played in preceding programmes to **trail ahead** to the documentary
- A **dry version** for podcasting (current **podcast** consumption stands at around eleven thousand downloads a week, so this is an important audience)
- A piece of visual for the London 1 website to be used for **viral marketing**

Format

There is now a variety of **formats** available to the producer. These are:
- Two five-minute **packages** and a studio discussion with two guests
- Two ten-minute packages
- One twenty-minute package

Content

All documentaries must be based on the highest journalistic standards and deal with the subject matter in an appropriate and interesting way. They should also, where possible, try to avoid being too serious. Their approach should be innovative and include interviews with people who are interesting and a little out of the ordinary. Editors should make use of all the tools that sound engineers have available. All programmes commissioned by London 1 will be subject to the relevant guidelines, including the Editorial Guidelines. Copies of these guidelines can be accessed on www.London1/info/guidelines.

Areas that London 1 is looking at for documentaries in the next four months

Music based: Madonna, Duffy, U2, Dr Dre, Coldplay, Green Day, Usher, Rick Rubin, Elbow.

Social issue based: The environment; World Aids Day; back to school / new beginning at school/university/work; life changes; how Christmas can be very stressful for lots of reasons: families, expectations, eating disorders, depression; there are also the recurrent themes of mental health, exam revision, and career decisions and choices.

Additional requirements

Details of **cues**, billings and support material are outlined in a separate document that can be accessed on London 1's commissioning website: www.London1/commissioning/

Price

The cost of a London 1 documentary is around £3,000, though some budgets are subject to foreign travel, and are likely to be higher.

The commissioning process

To formally submit a proposal, please complete the proposal by midnight, 16 May. The Commissioning Team intends to communicate commissioning decisions by the beginning of June, and we plan the documentaries to **go on air** from August through until early next year. We aim to give feedback to everyone who submits a proposal.

c **Read the commissioning brief on page 20 again and answer the following questions.**

1 Who listens to London 1?
2 Apart from the audio documentary, what else does the producer have to provide?
3 How many different formats can the producer choose from?
4 What kind of documentaries do London 1 want to commission?
5 Why are two web links included?
6 What is the budget for a London 1 documentary?
7 When is the deadline for proposals?
8 When will the documentaries be broadcast?

d **Complete the following definitions using the words in bold in the commissioning brief.**

1 A pre-recorded radio item which can include all or some of the following things: interviews, comments, music: _package_
2 Length and structure: _____
3 A digital medium that is distributed over the Internet and can be listened to on a personal computer or portable media player: _____
4 A pre-recorded item which includes only the spoken word – that is, no music or sound effects: _____
5 Words said by a DJ/presenter to introduce and link segments/music: _____
6 Most important listeners: _____
7 To promote with a preview: _____
8 To be broadcast: _____
9 A technique that uses established social networks to promote a product; for example, friends forwarding a funny video clip by email: _____

e **In groups, discuss the following questions.**

1 If you were to produce a documentary for London 1, which of the topics mentioned in the brief would you choose? Explain why.
2 If you were to commission a documentary for a national radio station in your country, what subject would you commission it about? Explain why.

f **Write the introductory cues for the documentaries you discussed in Exercise 2e. Use the language in Exercise 1e to help you.**

Understanding the production process

3 a **Read the following statements about radio. Number the statements from 1 to 5: 1 = strongly agree, 5 = strongly disagree.**

☐ Radio is an out-of-date way of receiving news and listening to music.
☐ The quality of radio programmes is higher if the radio is state-funded.
☐ All radio DJs/presenters are waiting for the opportunity to be on TV.
☐ Everybody prefers the TV to the radio.
☐ Young people no longer listen to the radio.

b **In pairs, compare and discuss your answers.**

c Complete the definitions (1–11) using the words in the word web.

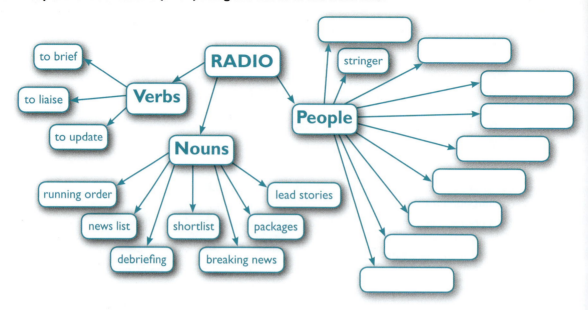

1 List chosen from a longer list: ___shortlist___
2 Sequence of stories in a radio show: _____
3 Events that are happening as we speak: _____
4 The most important stories: _____
5 To give instructions/information: _____
6 Stories to be included in a programme: _____
7 Pre-recorded radio items which contain interviews, comments, music, etc.:
_____
8 A freelance journalist: _____
9 Detailed discussion about work that has been done: _____
10 To add the most recent information: _____
11 To speak to people in order to exchange information with them:
_____

d *To brief* and *to update* can also be used as nouns – *a brief, an update.*
   Which of the nouns in the word web can also be used as verbs?

e The magazine extract on page 23 is from a profile of Dawn Henderson, a
   producer for the current affairs radio show *Good Morning Australia*. The
   profile was published in an Australian magazine in an article from a series
   called *A Day in the Life of* ... Complete Dawn's typical 24-hour schedule
   using terms in the word web in Exercise 3c.

9 AM

Arrive at work. Read all the newspapers, check breaking news on satellite. Start preparing (1) _____news list_____ .

11 AM

Morning meeting with editor, deputy editor, broadcast journalists and researchers to discuss news list and decide (2) _____ for tomorrow's programme.

11.30 AM

In newsroom, tell reporters and researchers who to interview for research and who to invite to tomorrow's programme. Contact (3) _____ if necessary. Decide (4) _____ of programme.

12–4 PM

Afternoon news meeting with staff from morning meeting and overnight producer, journalists and researchers to tell them which stories will be (5) _____ and which will be dropped, and which scripts need to be written.

4–7 PM

Listen to (6) _____ for show. Edit as necessary. Speak to presenters on phone to (7) _____ them about running order of programme. Keep in regular contact with journalists and researchers. Solve any problems that occur. Change focus of news items if necessary.

7 PM–3 AM

At home. Watch evening news and late news to be aware of any (8) _____ .

3 AM

Return to work. Check news again. Check running order, scripts and audios. Give new stories to reporters on duty if necessary.

5 AM

Talk presenters through show: explain the script and who does which interviews.

6–9 AM

On air. (9) _____ news list to react to breaking news. Deal with guests who are late or don't arrive. (10) _____ with studio manager to check outside broadcast lines are OK. Speak to reporters about what you want them to say during interviews.

9 AM

(11) _____ . Discuss what worked and didn't work on the show. Email debriefing note to overnight staff.

9.30 AM

Sort out accounts: payments for taxis, guests, etc. Go home.

f **Would you like to do Dawn Henderson's job? Explain why / why not.**

g **Complete the 'People' section of the word web in Exercise 3c using words in the extract in Exercise 3e. Can you add any more vocabulary to the word web?**

h **In pairs, discuss whether you think word webs are a good way to learn vocabulary. How do *you* learn vocabulary? Compare your ideas.**

4 a ▶ **2.3 Listen to Dawn Henderson giving instructions in the newsroom. Which of the following items does she mention and in what order?**

☐ Children's names ☐ Rising house prices
☐ Schools closing ☐ World War II
☐ Global warming ☐ A new museum

b ▶2.3 Listen again and tick (✓) the phrases that you hear.

A
Can/could you deal with ... ?
I want you to ...
I'd like a(n) ...
I'd like you to ...
Speak to ...
Use ...
Contact ...
Would you mind ... ?
Will you ... ?
You'll need to ...

B
Do you mean ... ?
Shall I ... ?
Should I ... ?

c Choose the best title for columns A and B in Exercise 4b from the following list. Write the titles in the table.

- Checking editorial content
- Checking instructions
- Giving instructions
- Managing an editorial meeting

d Which phrases in column A are the most direct and which are the most indirect? What effect can using direct and indirect instructions like this have?

e Complete the following table using the phrases in Exercise 4b that are followed by a noun, a gerund (*-ing*) or by the infinitive. Look at Audioscript 2.3 on page 93 to help you.

+ noun or person	+ gerund	+ infinitive
Can/could you deal with the piece about ...		

f Correct the mistakes in the following sentences.

1 Shall I to use our contacts database?
2 I like a five-minute package on that story.
3 I'd like you briefing the guests thoroughly.
4 I want you liaise with our stringer in San Francisco.
5 Could you mind checking the story for accuracy?

g In groups, role play a meeting to decide the content for a radio package about learning English in your country. Use your own ideas and the notes to help you. Student A, you are the producer; Student B, you are a researcher; and Student C, you are a reporter. Swap roles and practise again. Make sure each student has a chance to be the producer.

Possible ideas for 'Learning English' package.

* Why is learning English important?
* Is English taught at school? What ages? How many hours? Interview: teachers/educationalists/parents.
* Do private English schools exist? Who is their market? Young learners, adults, business people, other? Interview private language school owner.
* What other ways of learning English are there? Private lessons, other?
* Are initiatives for learning English successful? Why / why not? Interview a selection of learners giving their views.
* Other?

Planning a news list

5 a **In groups, discuss the following questions.**

1 If you had to make a news list for a thirty-minute current affairs programme tomorrow morning, which six stories would you include? Explain why.

2 What would be the running order?

b **Look at the box below. It contains some vocabulary taken from Dawn Henderson's news list for the first thirty minutes of *Good Morning Australia*, which you heard being discussed in Audio 2.3. For each story, there are two words/phrases. Guess which pairs of words/phrases are from the same story, and discuss what you think each story will be about.**

> World War II   schools   homeless shelter   global warming   names   house prices
> cruelty   honour   museum   estate agent   birth rate   overhyped

I think 'estate agent' and 'house prices' are from the same story. It will probably be about how expensive it is to buy a house these days.

c **Read the news list to see if your predictions were correct.**

News list, 29 January

1 **House prices in Australia are continuing to rise, estate agents have announced**.
Interview an estate agent and prepare a package with a first-time buyer explaining how difficult it is to get on the housing ladder.

2 **Schools in rural areas are struggling to stay open because of a falling birth rate, which means there is not enough funding**.
Local authorities are being told to re-organise schools, but this inevitably means some schools will close, which will cause big protests. What can be done about the situation? Speak to a leading educationalist and parents involved with a protest group to keep their local school open.

3 **Does global warming exist?**
The recent fires all over Australia are just the latest event to be blamed on global warming, but another group of scientists believes the phenomenon is overhyped, and that this is just how the Earth should be reacting. Speak to *Friends of the Earth* and a leading meteorologist.

4 **Following the announcement of the latest strange name for a celebrity child, should parents who give their children ridiculous names be labelled as cruel?**
Get a child psychologist and an adult who has a strange name to discuss whether they have suffered (or not) because of their name.

5 **Campaigners want to honour a boy from Alice Springs**.
He is believed to be the youngest Australian killed who fought in World War II. Interview campaigners and the family.

6 **Yet another Picasso museum has been opened in France**.
Furthermore, it's in a building which was previously used as a night shelter for homeless people. More art or more heart? Talk to a representative of the museum and someone from the homeless shelter.

d **In pairs, discuss which of the stories from the news list you would most, and least, like to research and write. Explain why.**

e Look at the sentences in **bold** in the news list and decide if the following statements are True (T) or False (F).

> **topic sentence** (*noun*)
> the sentence in a paragraph that summarises the main idea of the paragraph.

1   These sentences summarise the topic of the item.
2   They are all examples of topic sentences.
3   The topic sentence is always controversial.
4   All the topic sentences in this news list use present tenses.
5   Topic sentences are never questions.

f Underline the topic sentences in the following news list items.

1   Is the Liberal Party leader too old to win the general election? A recent poll shows that many young voters do not even know his name and when shown his photo, think he is too old for the job. Record a package asking a wide range of people what they think. Get a representative from *Age Concern* and a spokesperson from the Liberal party.
2   Top universities are still failing to attract large numbers of students from state schools. Speak to the dean of a top university and teachers from a private and a state school.
3   It's Oscar time again, but are the Oscars valid, or just another marketing ploy? Interview people in the film sector and prepare a package of previous Oscar film winners.

g Look at the extract below from the *Good Morning Australia* news list and answer the following questions.

> Interview an estate agent and prepare a package with a first-time buyer explaining how difficult it is to get on the housing ladder.

1   Is the producer explaining the story or explaining how to develop the story?
2   What is the underlined verb form?
3   Why is this verb form used?

h Write a news list for a thirty-minute current affairs programme tomorrow morning, using the ideas you discussed in Exercise 5a. Remember to use topic sentences and to give clear instructions using the imperative.

6 a ▶2.4 **Listen to a phone conversation between Dawn Henderson and Sarah Bernard, a stringer. Complete Sarah's notes.**

Story – new Picasso museum in France

Write – 1)
            2)

People to interview – 1)
                      2)

Fee –

Deadline –

b ▶2.4 **Many words and phrases in English have alternatives which mean more or less the same thing. Below are some useful phrases for briefing someone over the phone, which illustrate this point. Listen to Dawn and Sarah's conversation again and underline the alternative that you hear. Both alternatives are correct. Does the meaning of any of the sentences change depending on which word you use?**

1 I'm calling you **as**/**because** we **need**/want a story for tomorrow's programme about the new Picasso museum in France.
2 I **want**/**need** you to write me a short script outlining the issues ...
3 **You also need** / **You'll also need** to write interview questions and brief them on what we'll ask.
4 **They'll be needed** / **They are needed** on air between 6 and 7 am Australian time.
5 **Could**/**Can** you do it, and are you interested?
6 The payment **will be** / **is** the standard fee.
7 When do you **need**/want the story for?
8 **We'll need** / **We need** the script and contact numbers by 4 pm our time at the latest.

c **In pairs, role play a phone call between a producer and a stringer. Use the news list you wrote in Exercise 5h and the phrases in Exercise 6b to help you.**

Giving post-production feedback

7 a **In pairs, discuss the following questions.**
1 Do you ever take part in debriefing meetings for your work? What is discussed in your debriefing meetings?
2 Do you think debriefing meetings are useful? Explain why / why not.

b **Look at the following points, which might be mentioned in a debriefing meeting for a radio programme. Decide if the points are positive (P) or negative (N).**
☐ A booked speaker does not arrive for the show   N
☐ Research not done well
☐ Being first with breaking news
☐ Studio going down for several seconds
☐ Getting an eyewitness report for a breaking news story
☐ Interviewees not briefed well

c ▶2.5 **Listen to a debriefing meeting at the *Good Morning Australia* studio and tick (✓) the points in Exercise 7b that they discuss.**

d ▶2.5 **Listen again and complete the following extracts.**

1 Who wants ____to____ ___comment___ first on this morning's show?
2 … the show being off air was not a _____ _____ .
3 We're still trying to figure out _____ _____ .
4 Do you have any idea what the _____ _____ and how we can avoid it _____ _____ in the future?
5 … what _____ _____ the meteorology expert?
6 … getting an eyewitness _____ of the rail crash was a _____ scoop.
7 I was also very _____ _____ the piece about house prices, and I think the piece on the Picasso museum was _____ _____ .

e In groups of four, role play a debriefing meeting. Student A, you are the producer; Student B, you are the technical expert; Students C and D, you are researchers. Student A, read the notes below and prepare to lead the meeting; Students B, C and D, be prepared to explain and/or justify the points below that you were responsible for.

> Notes for debriefing meeting
>
> * We were the first to report the resignation of the Prime Minister.
>
> * The quality of the outdoor broadcast for the piece on the opening of a new train station was very poor.
>
> * Inaccurate research for the piece on a possible cure for cancer made the presenter look ill-informed when interviewing the expert.
>
> * The guest booked to talk about new Australian writers arrived two hours late.

8 **a** Read the extract from the debriefing meeting in Audio 2.5 and answer the following questions.

… the studio <u>going down</u> for several seconds, and the show being off air was not a great moment. We're still trying to <u>figure out</u> what happened.

1 Which <u>underlined</u> verb means *understand* and which means *stop working*?
2 What do the underlined verbs have in common?

b Decide if the following statements are True (T) or False (F).

1 Phrasal verbs are verbs followed by particles such as *in, out, off* or *away*.
2 The meaning of phrasal verbs is always literal.
3 A phrasal verb has only one meaning.
4 When you check the meaning of a phrasal verb in the dictionary, you should check the verb entry, not the entry for the particle.

c Complete the following phrases that a radio DJ or presenter might say, using the phrasal verbs in the box.

> coming up   go over   lined up   moving on   run out of   wind up

1 _____ to our next story, ...
2 _____ later, all the showbiz gossip, but first, let's _____ to the newsroom for ...
3 What do we have _____ on the show today?
4 I'm afraid we're going to have to _____ the interview there, as we've _____ time.

d Use your dictionary to complete the following sentences using phrasal verbs formed from the words in brackets.

1 When you hear a good song on the radio, do you ___turn up___ the volume? (turn)
2 Have you _____ to any new radio stations recently? Which ones? (tune)
3 Do you think journalists ever _____ stories? How do they _____ it? (make; get)
4 Do you think the government should _____ money to fund public radio stations? How much? (set)
5 Could you _____ radio? What would you listen to instead? (do)

e In pairs, ask and answer the questions in Exercise 8d.

9 **a** The following text is the debriefing email that Dawn Henderson sent to the overnight staff (who were not present at the debriefing meeting) to tell them how the show went. Which four points does Dawn comment on?

> Thank you for all your efforts on this morning's programme.
>
> Starting with the bad news: the studio went down for several seconds. Jim and his team are still trying to figure out why this happened. Hopefully they'll have some answers very soon. The meteorologist failed to show up for the global warming story, so I think we should avoid using him again in the future.
>
> On a positive note, we did really well on the rail crash story – we managed to get an eyewitness account as soon as the news broke. (Unfortunately it wasn't us who broke the news!) And Sarah Bernard – the stringer in France – provided a great script and two radio-friendly guests for the Picasso museum piece.
>
> Dawn

b In pairs, answer the following questions.

1 Does the email summarise the debriefing meeting successfully?
2 Does the email suggest action to be taken?
3 What opening and closing salutations does Dawn use?
4 Which phrases does Dawn use to introduce the negative and positive points?
5 Is the email formal or informal? (Is standard or non-standard English used? What punctuation is used?)

c Write a debriefing email for the debriefing meeting you held in Exercise 7e.

UNIT 3 Magazines

- Composing magazine covers
- Planning the contents of a magazine
- Giving instructions for a photo shoot
- Planning and writing a true-life story

Composing magazine covers

1 a In pairs, discuss the following questions.

1 Which magazines do you read? Why do you read them?
2 What are the most popular magazines in your country at the moment? Why do you think they are the most popular?
3 What do you find difficult about reading magazines in English?

b Look at the English-language magazine covers at the top of the page. Decide which of the magazines you would most/least like to read. Explain why / why not.

c Find the following things on the cover.

> title   price   ~~issue number~~   date   bar code
> coverline   slogan

d In pairs, discuss which parts of a magazine cover are the most influential in making you buy a magazine. Explain why.

e Look at the magazine titles in the box and answer the following questions.

> Vogue   Simply Knitting   Cosmopolitan   FHM
> What Car?   GQ   House Beautiful   Esquire
> Glamour   PS3   Beautiful Britain   T3

1 Which titles give information about content?
2 Which titles suggest a type of person or lifestyle?
3 Which titles give no obvious information about their content or readers?

2 **a** Match the coverlines (1–8) to the kinds of magazine below (a–e). There may be more than one possible answer.

> **coverline** (noun)
> short lines of text on the front cover of magazines which try to get the reader's interest by describing some of the articles in the magazine

1 Get ready for RIO:
fabulous funky fashions

2 **The most amazing year EVER?**
"I met my prince charming, got my dream job, gave birth to triplets and won the lottery!"

3 **No TV ever!**
Is it time to impose a total ban for toddlers?

4 **Make your house clean & green!**

5 Get *fit* and *fabulous*!
The best exercises for brides-to-be!

6 *Beat the heat:*
great summer fashion

7 **The ten best guys' books you'll ever read!!!**

8 **Shape up & show off**
Get bikini ready – FAST!

a women's magazine
b men's magazine
c parenting magazine
d house magazine
e wedding magazine

b In pairs, discuss the following questions about magazine coverlines. Use the examples in Exercise 2a to help you. (You will check your answers in Exercise 2c.)

1 Can underlining, **bolding**, CAPITALISATION, font size and style, and colour vary?
2 Is it impolite to use imperatives in coverlines?
3 What punctuation is omitted in coverlines?
4 What part of an article is sometimes introduced by quotation marks in coverlines?
5 Is it OK to use questions in coverlines?

c Match the questions in Exercise 2b (1–5) to the answers below (a–e).

a No, not all. In fact, they are very common, especially in celebrity magazines, magazines aimed at young people and young adults, and magazines with a more populist appeal (e.g. in *Glamour* but not *Vogue*, in *FHM* but not in *Esquire*); they try to involve the reader directly.

b Full stops are often omitted, but other punctuation is used. Exclamation marks are a common feature of coverlines (especially in celebrity magazines, magazines aimed at young people and young adults, and magazines with a more populist appeal) because they show emotion and immediacy, and increase involvement.

c Yes. Good use of typographical features is an important way of getting the reader's attention.

d Yes. The idea is that the reader will want to read the article to find the answer.

e Sometimes there is a direct quotation from the interviewee which includes the most sensational part of the story (especially in celebrity magazines, magazines aimed at young people and young adults, and magazines with a more populist appeal).

d Look at the coverlines (1–6) and identify the features listed in Exercises 2b and c.

1 **What men REALLY want in life** (you'll be surprised!)

2 **316** really brilliant fashion finds

3 **Need $ fast?**
Follow our 7-day smart earner plan

4 *"Kidnapped by a man I met on the Net"*

5 **Spanish special:**
tasty tapas recipes and magical Madrid gourmet guide

6 **Quick and easy flowering gardens**

3 a ▶3.1 Listen to a radio advertisement for a magazine and decide which kind of magazine it is.

b Look at the two coverlines you just heard in Exercise 3a (a and b) and answer the following questions.

1 Which coverline uses rhyming words?
2 Which coverline uses alliteration (words that begin with the same consonant sound)?

a *Beat the heat:*
great summer fashion

b **Shape up &** **show off**
Get bikini ready – FAST!

c Look at the following coverlines and decide which pronunciation features are used (rhyming and/or alliteration).

1 Make your house **clean** & **green**!

2 Get *fit* and *fabulous!*
The best exercise for brides-to-be!

3 **Spanish special:**
tasty tapas recipes and magical Madrid gourmet guide

4 **Fun in the sun:**
ten top holiday destinations

5 **Matt Damon's killer instinct:** why we prefer Bourne to Bond

6 **Beijing rising**

7 What to wear from **19** to **91**

d ▶3.2 Listen to the coverlines in Exercise 3c and check your answers. Practise saying the coverlines.

e In pairs, write suitable coverlines for the following magazine articles. Use the words in brackets to help you.

1 A famous actress, Julia Roberts, is photographed on a beach looking incredible. (*wow! / body secrets*) Wow! Julia's beach body secrets
2 A top Hollywood couple's romance is becoming more serious.
(*Jen and Paul / "She's fantastic!"*)
3 How to easily transform your garden. (*stunning / makeover / easier*)
4 A new diet to help you lose weight very quickly.
(*hottest / lose ten kilos / two months*)
5 How doing exercise can help you give up smoking. (*fit / quit / give up nicotine*)
6 A review of the best new cars of the year. (*coolest*)
7 The best guitar songs of all time. (*greatest / tracks*)

f Compare your coverlines with the suggested answers in the key on page 103. Which do you prefer?

Planning the contents of a magazine

4 a In pairs, make a list of the typical contents of magazines aimed at women aged between 25 and 45.

b ▶3.3 An editorial meeting is taking place to plan the next issue of *Glorious* magazine, a monthly magazine aimed at women aged between 25 and 45. Listen to two extracts from the meeting and see how many of your ideas from Exercise 4a are mentioned.

c ▶3.3 Listen again and answer the following questions.

1 According to the fashion editor, who are going to be big names in the future?
2 What does Scott want to commission a short piece about?
3 Why does the editor-in-chief say "I'll hand you over to Richard."?
4 What is Grace going to do a short piece about?
5 When are the deadlines for commissioning articles, copy and artwork?
6 When are the members of the editorial team meeting to make the final decision on contents for the July issue?

d <u>Underline</u> the verb forms used to express the future in the questions in Exercise 4c. Then decide which verb form is used in the following situations.

1 To express a spontaneous decision about the future
2 To talk about a plan for the future made before the moment of speaking
3 To talk about a fixed future arrangement
4 To talk about a future schedule
5 To make a prediction about the future

e Look at the following sentences from an editorial planning meeting and decide who might say them: the deputy editor, the fashion editor, the beauty editor, the picture editor, or all of them. There may be more than one possible answer.

1 I'll look into the new Chanel cosmetic range.

2 I'm meeting Peter tomorrow to decide which photos we want to use.

3 We're not going to include the story about student debt.

4 There's no way I'm going to meet the deadline.

5 What time is the Armani shoot?

f Look at the sentences in Exercise 4e again and decide which verb form has been used in each sentence to express the future. Explain why.

g Below are four excerpts from four different conversations. Complete the sentences using the most likely future tense of the verb in brackets.

1 I _____ _____ Matt Damon tomorrow. I'm so nervous! (*interview*)
2 Don't worry about the deadline. It's been extended. It _____ the 23rd, not the 19th. (*be*)
3 I _____ _____ the copy when I get back. (*proofread*)
4 I'd really like to know when I'_____ _____ _____ _____ ! (*be paid*)

h ▶3.4 Listen to the excerpts and check your answers.

5 a ▶3.5 Listen to the fashion editor's proposal from the editorial planning meeting again and tick (✓) the phrases that you hear.

Making and justifying a proposal	Making objections	Dealing with objections
I'd like to propose a piece on … , as …	I don't know.	That's not a problem.
I think a story about … would be really interesting.	I'm not sure if …	You don't need to worry about that because …
It might be expensive, but …	It sounds promising, but …	
I want to do an article on … because …		

b Imagine you work for a men's magazine. Think of three stories that would be good in the summer edition. Using the phrases in the first column above, plan how you will present your ideas at the editorial meeting.

c In groups of three, role play making and objecting to a proposal. Student A, make your proposals; Students B and C, make objections at the end; Student A, deal with their objections. Use the language in the table in Exercise 5a to help you. When you have finished, swap roles and practise again.

d ▶3.6 Listen to four more excerpts from the editorial planning meeting. Decide how each expression is being used.

1 To keep order
2 To hand over to somebody else
3 To sum up

e ▶3.6 Listen again and write the expressions you hear in the table below.

Keeping order	Handing over	Summing up
Let's keep it relevant.	Over to you, … I'll pass you over to … So, who's going to start?	To sum up, …

f In groups, role play an editorial meeting. Choose a real magazine that you are all familiar with. Student A, take the role of editor-in-chief; the others, take different roles in the magazine – you could choose from art director, fashion editor, photo editor, features editor, travel editor, or any other position. Agree on the contents for your next issue.

Giving instructions for a photo shoot

6 a **In pairs, discuss the following questions.**

1 How important are photographs to a magazine's success?
2 Do different kinds of magazine use different kinds of photo?
3 Have you ever used a photo library? If so, which one, and do you have a favourite photo library?
4 How do magazines commission photographers?

b **Read the two emails below and answer the following questions. Explain your answers.**

1 Do the emails contain the same information?
2 Which is the most informal?

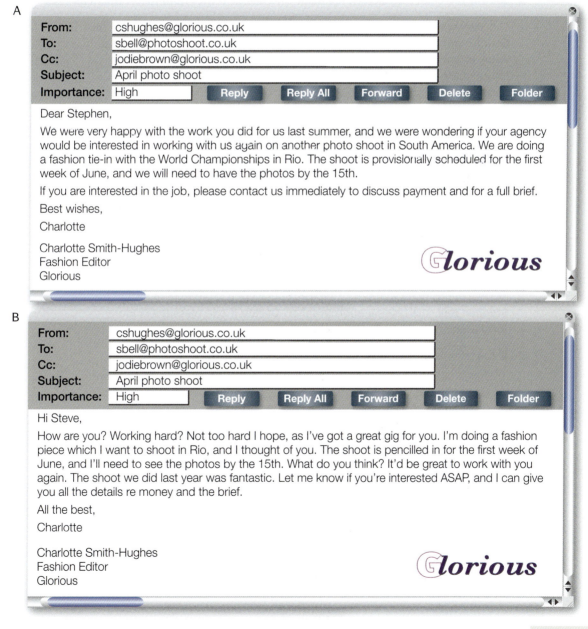

A

From:	cshughes@glorious.co.uk
To:	sbell@photoshoot.co.uk
Cc:	jodiebrown@glorious.co.uk
Subject:	April photo shoot
Importance:	High

Reply   Reply All   Forward   Delete   Folder

Dear Stephen,

We were very happy with the work you did for us last summer, and we were wondering if your agency would be interested in working with us again on another photo shoot in South America. We are doing a fashion tie-in with the World Championships in Rio. The shoot is provisionally scheduled for the first week of June, and we will need to have the photos by the 15th.

If you are interested in the job, please contact us immediately to discuss payment and for a full brief.

Best wishes,

Charlotte

Charlotte Smith-Hughes
Fashion Editor
Glorious

Glorious

B

From:	cshughes@glorious.co.uk
To:	sbell@photoshoot.co.uk
Cc:	jodiebrown@glorious.co.uk
Subject:	April photo shoot
Importance:	High

Reply   Reply All   Forward   Delete   Folder

Hi Steve,

How are you? Working hard? Not too hard I hope, as I've got a great gig for you. I'm doing a fashion piece which I want to shoot in Rio, and I thought of you. The shoot is pencilled in for the first week of June, and I'll need to see the photos by the 15th. What do you think? It'd be great to work with you again. The shoot we did last year was fantastic. Let me know if you're interested ASAP, and I can give you all the details re money and the brief.

All the best,

Charlotte

Charlotte Smith-Hughes
Fashion Editor
Glorious

Glorious

c When writing an email, there are some things you should always try to do and others you should never do. Complete the following statements about writing emails using either *Always* or *Never*.

1 ____Always____ put a subject line.
2 ____Never____ forget to check for grammar and spelling mistakes.
3 _____ choose the appropriate register (formal, neutral, informal).
4 _____ personalise your message to the recipient.
5 _____ forget your signature.
6 _____ try to keep your message short if you can.
7 _____ forward an email without permission.
8 _____ think that no one else will ever see your email.
9 _____ expect an immediate answer.

d Look at the emails in Exercise 6b again and decide if they both follow the rules.

e The statements in Exercise 6c are all examples of good email etiquette for both formal and informal emails. There are some features, however, that apply to only formal or informal emails. In pairs, decide if the following features are formal or informal, and then find examples in the emails.

1 Use of slang   *Informal (e.g. 'gig')*
2 Use of contractions
3 Use of *Dear* and *Best wishes*
4 Omitting words
5 Use of abbreviations

7 a In groups, discuss the following questions.

1 Do you prefer to send emails or speak over the phone?
2 Have you got an answering machine? If so, what is the recorded message?
3 How do you feel about leaving messages on answering machines?
4 Have you ever had to leave messages on an answering machine in English? Did you find it easy or difficult?

b ▶3.7 Listen to two examples of Charlotte leaving a telephone message for Stephen Bell, the fashion photographer. Decide if one message is more formal than the other. Explain your answer.

c ▶3.7 Listen again and complete the following extracts.

1 You're (a) ____through____ ____to____ the *Photo Shoot Agency*. We're sorry that nobody is able to take your call at the moment. Please leave a message and your details, and we'll (b) _____ _____ _____
_____ as soon as possible.

Hello. (c) _____ _____ Charlotte Smith-Hughes, the fashion editor of *Glorious* magazine. I'm calling to …
Could you please (d) _____ _____ _____ _____
0207 478274 to confirm …

2 Hi, this is Steve. I can't speak right now. (a) _____ _____
_____ _____ .

Hi, Steve. (b) _____ Charlotte … Give me (c) a _____ to confirm …
My work number is 0207 478274. Speak to you soon.

d Look at the answerphone messages in Exercise 7c. Change the information to write a recorded message for your work answer phone and one for your home phone.

e In pairs, practise leaving a message on an answerphone. Student A, read out your recorded message; Student B, leave a message asking the person who you are calling to phone you urgently regarding an important meeting. Swap roles and practise again.

8 a Read the extract from the brief for the World Championships fashion photo shoot in Rio. In pairs, discuss if you think the spread will be good. Explain why / why not.

Glorious

Photo shoot: World Championships
ref: 07/11fas

Context
Glorious is a glossy women's magazine. Its market is women in their mid-20s to mid-40s. It has a young, dynamic feel. It includes sections on beauty, health and fitness, romance, work, fashion, travel and culture, as well as true-life stories.

Brief
This is a high-cost shoot and will be the principal fashion spread and focus for the World Championships theme in the July issue. The spread will be ten pages.

This spread has two objectives:

1) to capture the innovation and originality of the new breed of fashion designers that are currently emerging in Rio

2) to draw on the beauty of locations in Rio.

The photos must showcase the work of new, young designers within their own vibrant culture. We want the shoot to be dynamic and colourful, combining the city's rich history with its modern side.

Timescale
Date of shoot: 5th June
Deadline for photos: 15th June

Fee
The fee for the two-day shoot is £1,000.

Contact
Charlotte Smith-Hughes
Fashion editor
Glorious
cshughes@glorious.co.uk
0207 478274

---

b Complete the following definitions using the headings in **bold** in the brief.

1 Payment: _____
2 Deadline(s): _____
3 Background: _____
4 Communication: _____
5 Requirements: _____

c Answer the following questions about the brief by choosing the correct alternative (a or b).

1 The Context section describes
  a the magazine.
  b the shoot.

2 The Context section uses
  a the present simple.
  b the present continuous.

3 The Brief section describes
  a the magazine.
  b the shoot.

4 The Brief section uses
  a mostly present tenses, *may* and *should*
  b a combination of present simple, *must* and *will*

d Imagine you are the editor-in-chief of your school/company magazine. For the next issue, you have commissioned an article about new members of staff (or another current topic), and you would like a photo spread to accompany the article. Write a photo shoot brief, using the brief in Exercise 8a as a model.

Planning and writing a true-life story

9 a In groups, discuss the following questions.

1 What kinds of magazine include true stories in their features sections?
2 Why do you think some people like reading true stories?
3 Do you like reading true stories? Explain why / why not.
4 What makes people tell stories about their private lives to a journalist?

b Most true stories in magazines can be divided into the following four sections. Write the following section headings in the notebook below in the order you would expect them to appear.

a Moral (the lesson of the story)
b Problem
c Setting (characters, place, time)
d Solution

c You are going to read an article called *Lightning strikes twice*. Match the notes the journalist made (a–f) to the correct headings on the right (1–4).

a Matt has to have a liver transplant and then his wife Ann has to have a liver transplant.
b This experience, which often causes couples to separate, has made Ann and Matt stronger and care for each other more.
c Ann and Matt
d The story starts when Matt is 39.
e Both Matt and Ann have successful operations.
f The USA

d Think of a true story. It could be personal, about people you know, or invented. Make notes like those in Exercise 9c.

Lightning strikes twice

1 _____

2 _____

3 _____

4 _____

Lightning strikes twice

When her husband told her the awful news, she had no idea there would be more to come.

Ann Storm felt nervous at work that day. She was worried about her husband Matt's doctor's appointment that afternoon. When she got home that evening, she went into their bedroom. Matt was waiting for her, his eyes full of tears.

"What?" she shouted in a panic. "What did the doctor say?"

Matt managed to say, "I need a liver transplant; without it I will die." He was 39 years old.

> ❝ **I need a liver transplant, without it I will die** ❞

After months of waiting, a donor liver became available. Matt and Ann held hands tightly as they drove up the motorway to the hospital. They were still holding hands as Matt was wheeled into the operating room at 3 am. "I might not survive this," Matt thought. As Ann kissed her husband goodbye, they both cried.

The operation went well, and he was soon back at home. Four months after the transplant, Matt was begging to return to work. He had read 36 books and watched every programme on TV. "I had more energy than ever," he remembers. "Life was looking good again."

Then, two years later, Ann suddenly fainted at work. She was taken to hospital, where tests showed Ann had suffered liver failure. A brutally honest doctor said that Ann could die at any time.

Now it was Ann's turn to wait for a donor liver. The Storms were not optimistic. "Two livers for one family?" Ann wondered. In August they decided to return to the Greek island of Kefalonia, where they'd honeymooned ten years earlier. "We knew this could be our last time together and were determined to enjoy it," says Matt. "We just wanted to be together," explains Ann. "That was the most important thing."

It was a shock when, a few weeks after they returned from Kefalonia, a call came from the hospital. Matt drove his wife to Glasgow "like a maniac", and saw the helicopter with the donor liver arrive on the hospital roof. The operation finished at seven the next morning. She left the hospital after ten days.

> ❝ **We just wanted to be with each other** ❞

Before Matt's transplant, Ann received a call from a nurse asking how long the Storms had been married, and if they really loved each other. "Why are you asking all these questions?" Ann responded. "Because," the nurse told her, "the transplant experience is so stressful that some couples split up." It has been just the opposite for the Storms.

At the end of a Friday night meal at a local restaurant, Matt urges Ann to put her coat on. "It's cold out there." Ann puts on her coat, and Matt puts his arm around her. "That's the way it is," Matt adds as they go out into the winter night. As long as we're together, we can weather any storm."

b Without looking back at the article, complete the following sentences using the verbs in the box. Then put the sentences in the correct order.

> became   felt   finished   had suffered   left   managed   puts (x2)   was   ~~was waiting~~

- ☐ Matt ___was waiting___ for her, his eyes full of tears.
- ☐ Now it _____ Ann's turn to wait for a donor liver.
- ☐ Ann Storm _____ nervous at work.
- ☐ Ann _____ on her coat, and Matt _____ his arm around her.
- ☐ A donor liver _____ available.
- ☐ The operation _____ at seven the next morning. She _____ the hospital after ten days.
- ☐ Matt _____ to say, "I need a liver transplant."
- ☐ Tests showed Ann _____ liver failure.

c Complete the following table using the name of the correct tense. Choose from past continuous, past perfect or past simple. Then find an example in the sentences in Exercise 10b.

Tense	Use	Example
Present simple	To bring a story into the present so that it seems more relevant and up-to-date	Ann puts on her coat, and Matt puts his arm around her.
	To narrate past events in a story in chronological order	
	To express duration or repetition in the past	
	To narrate an action that happened in the past before another past action	

d Without looking back at the article, complete the following excerpt from *Lightning strikes twice* using the correct past tense form of the verbs in brackets.

The operation ____went____ (go) well, and he _____ (be) soon back at home. Four months after the transplant, Matt _____ (beg) to return to work. He _____ (read) 36 books and _____ (watch) every programme on TV. "I had more energy than ever," he remembers. "Life was looking good again."

Then, two years later, Ann suddenly _____ (faint) at work. She was taken to hospital, where tests showed Ann _____ (suffer) liver failure. A brutally honest doctor said that Ann _____ (can) die at any time.

e Complete the following excerpts from *Lightning strikes twice* using the correct form of the following verbs. There may be more than one possible answer, but try to remember which verb was used in the actual article.

> tell   add   respond   ~~shout~~   explain   say

1 "What?" she ___shouted___ in a panic. "What did the doctor say?"
2 Matt managed to _____ , "I need a liver transplant; without it I will die."
3 "Why are you asking all these questions?" Ann _____ .

4 "Because," the nurse _____ her, "the transplant experience is so stressful that some couples split up."

5 "We just wanted to be together," _____ Ann. "That was all that mattered."

6 "That's the way it is," Matt _____ as they go out into the winter night. "As long as we're together, we can weather any storm."

f Read the article again and check your answers.

g The sentences in Exercise 10e use the reporting verbs *shout*, *say*, *respond*, *tell*, *explain* and *add*. Look at the article again and try to find more examples of reporting verbs.

h Cross out the incorrect words in the following statements. Use the examples in Exercise 10e to help you.

1 Direct speech [can/cannot] be used to interrupt the story, to give attention to a specific event or relationship, to show a character's personality, and to show relationships between characters.

2 [*Tell/Say*] is always followed by a direct personal pronoun or the name of a person, e.g. *He _____ her/Jane (that)* ...

3 [*Tell/Say*] cannot be followed by a direct personal pronoun, e.g. *He _____ (that)* ... or *He _____ to her/Jane (that)* ...

i The following phrases could all have been included in *Lightning strikes twice*. Complete the phrases using the verbs in the box. There may be more than one possible answer.

said told explained added

1 "I might not survive this," Matt thought. He _____ "I'd had five uncles who died from liver disease."

2 Instead of sitting in the waiting room alone, Ann spent an hour in the hospital chapel. Praying is a practice she's since made part of her daily life. "I hadn't prayed for years," she _____ , "but I prayed hard. Now I pray three times a day, every day."

3 A very honest doctor _____ Ann to "live for today because there might not be a tomorrow".

4 The Storms' love for each other has grown. "It's a whole new commitment," _____ Matt. "We're best friends."

11 a Write an article for a magazine, using the notes that you made for Exercise 9d. When you have finished, read your article and correct any mistakes. Give your article a good, catchy title.

b In groups, read the articles you have written and decide in which kind of magazine each article should be published.

UNIT 4 Television

- Understanding the pre-production process
- Organising a filming schedule
- Filming on location
- Editing a TV documentary

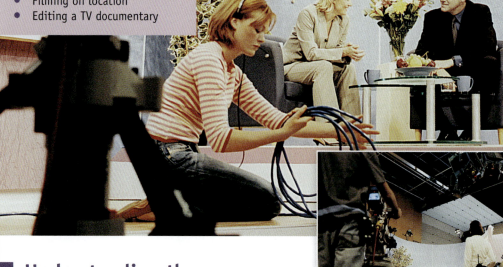

Understanding the pre-production process

1 a **In pairs, discuss the following questions.**

1 Do you work, or do you know anyone who works, in the TV industry? Describe what you/they do.
2 Would you like to work in the TV industry? Explain why / why not.
3 Look at some of the job titles used in the British TV industry: director of news and current affairs, editor, social affairs correspondent, reporter, researcher. Do the same jobs exist in your country? What are their responsibilities?
4 What differences do you think there are between being a newspaper journalist and being a TV journalist?

b ▶4.1 **Listen to a meeting about planning the agenda for a news broadcast at the *Scottish Broadcasting Corporation* (*SBC*). Which items are they going to run with (choose) for the evening's news broadcast?**

c ▶4.1 **Listen again and decide if the following statements are True (T) or False (F).**

1 Last night's story on the Prime Minister was very good.
2 The Asia correspondent is currently in India.
3 The police raided a building in Glasgow.
4 They will be able to get a Scottish angle on the trafficking story.
5 They would like to produce a whole programme about human trafficking.
6 They are going to meet again at two o'clock.

d Match the terms from Audio 4.1 (1–7) to their meanings (a–g).

1	correspondent	a	national and international press agencies, e.g. Associated Press, Reuters, Agence France
2	running order	b	a team responsible for filming
		c	recorded images shot on a digital video camera, often taken by eyewitnesses to news events
3	(a) live	d	the list of stories that make up a news programme
4	wires	e	a report from a reporter, usually from the scene of a breaking news story
5	(an) exclusive	f	a journalist employed by a TV station or a newspaper to report on a particular subject or send reports from a foreign country; similar to a reporter
6	DV footage		
7	camera crew	g	news which no other news organisation has

e Circle the word that does **not** collocate in each group.

		a		b		c	
1	**live**	a	footage	b	show	c	crew
2	**TV**	a	programme	b	live	c	channel
3	**exclusive**	a	director	b	story	c	footage
4	**camera**	a	work	b	crew	c	broadcast
5	**editing**	a	team	b	show	c	room
6	**news**	a	story	b	programme	c	top
7	**running**	a	order	b	commentary	c	crew
8	**live**	a	camera	b	coverage	c	broadcast

2

a In pairs, discuss the following questions.

1 Which of the following people are members of the production team?
 • editor • newsreader • reporter • researcher • camera operator
 • director-general

2 What is the role of the production team?

3 Have you ever worked in a production team? If so, describe what you did.

b ▶4.2 *SBC* has decided to start the new series of their current affairs programme, *Bird's Eye View*, with a documentary about human trafficking in Europe. The team are having a meeting to discuss how they will make the programme. Listen to the meeting and tick (✓) the things that they discuss.

☐ Research ☐ Filming
☐ Money ☐ Travel arrangements
☐ Interviews ☐ Advertising

c ▶4.2 Complete the following sentences using information from the meeting.

1 The ___pitch___ for the trafficking documentary has been approved.
2 The social affairs correspondent is going to help with some _____ research.
3 The _____ include lots of useful footage and interviews.
4 They agree to write a _____ based on the secondary research.
5 They want to avoid having too many _____ so the story will be more visually interesting.
6 The footage of the border posts will be taken from the _____ of a person being smuggled.

d Turn to page 95 and look at the underlined phrases in Audioscript 4.2, which all contain verbs which express modality. Complete the following table by writing the verbs from the audioscript in the correct column.

Possibility	Ability	Giving advice/ recommendation	Necessary	Not necessary
could				

e In the following sentences, both of the verbs in brackets are correct. However, one of the alternatives in each sentence has a deliberate mistake. Correct the mistakes so that both are correct.

1 The editor thinks you (*ought to* / *should to*) interview the film festival organisers.
should ~~to~~

2 We (*must to* / *have to*) get a package and a live from our New York correspondent.

3 The cameraman says he (*has better* / *should*) get footage of the setting before we arrive.

4 Jim is still an inexperienced reporter; he (*need to* / *must*) be told what news to write about.

5 We (*could* / *might to*) get an exclusive if we don't waste any time.

f In groups, role play a pre-production meeting, taking the roles of the people who normally attend such meetings: the director of news and current affairs, the editor, the social affairs correspondent, the reporter and the camera operator. Plan the agenda for a news broadcast, including anything you find particularly interesting in the news at the moment. Then choose a topic worth dedicating a whole programme to and discuss the necessary pre-production process.

Organising a filming schedule

3 **a** The team at *SBC* are preparing to make their documentary about human trafficking. In pairs, discuss the following questions.

1 What do you think the preparation will involve?
2 What roles do the editor and production manager play in the preparatory phase of a current affairs documentary or a TV series?
3 How many people do you think are involved in shooting on location?
4 Why is it important to have a filming schedule? What would you expect this schedule to include?

b Read the filming schedule for the *Bird's Eye View* shoot on page 45 and answer the following questions.

1 How long will the shoot last?
2 Where will the shoot take place?
3 Who are the people that are going to be interviewed?

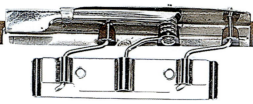

SBC News & Current Affairs　　　　*Bird's Eye View* Series 3

PSC FILMING SCHEDULE

WEEK:　　　　43
DATES:　　　　Monday 22 – Sunday 28 October
LOCATION:　　Various locations in Lindovia
TX DATE:　　TBC

CREW ON LOCATION

EDITOR:　　　Donna Eery　　　　086542 109 458
REPORTER:　　Neil Wax　　　　　086542 216 984
CAMERA:　　　James McCoy　　　07444 8731 4968
FIXER:　　　Stefan Manailescu　00 373 998 45629

TECHNICAL REQUIREMENTS

CAMERA	SOUND	LIGHTS
STANDARD **DIGIBETA** PSC	STANDARD **SCU** KIT	BASIC KIT
DIRECTOR TO PROVIDE **TAPE STOCK**		
CHECKLIST PRE-TRAVEL		
Flight Tickets, Foreign Currency & **Daily Rates**, **Release Forms**, **Carnets**, Passports, Visas, Excess Baggage Vouchers, Production Mobile, **Digital MP3 recorder**		

TRAVEL DAY

Monday 22 October

24.00　　Arrive airport. Taxi to hotel.

FILMING SCHEDULE

Tuesday 23 October

9.00　　**R/V** at Ministry to complete accreditation. Travel to Kotnasi.
　　　　IV girl who's suing her traffickers.
12.00　　Film **GVs** at the refuge. IV with psychologist and IVs with other victims of trafficking.
15.00　　**PTC**.
18.00　　R/V with representative from *Men Alone* organisation.

Wednesday 24 October

14.00　　IV National Coordinator for *Combating Human Trafficking* organisation.
16.00　　Travel to border – 120km. Film **sequences** and GVs at border.

Thursday 25 October

9.00　　R/V with IOM (*International Organisation for Migration*) Representative.
11.00　　Travel to location for IV with IOM Representative and PTC.
14.00　　Taxi back to capital

c Read the filming schedule again and answer the following questions.

1 Who do you think it was written by?
2 Who is it written for?
3 What kind of document is it? There may be more than one possible answer.
   - factual - friendly - informal - informative
4 What verb form is mainly used?
   - gerund (e.g. *doing*) - infinitive with *to* (e.g. *to do*)
   - infinitive without *to* (e.g. *do*)

d Complete the following definitions using the abbreviations in **bold** in the filming schedule in Exercise 3b.

1 Portable Single Camera; this means there is just one cameraman/woman responsible for recording both video and sound: _____PSC_____
2 Piece to camera; this is when a reporter speaks directly to the viewers through the camera: _____
3 Transmission date – that is, the day the finished programme will be broadcast: _____
4 Rendezvous – that is, to meet up with someone: _____
5 Interview: _____
6 General views; a series of shots of a location that are used to set the scene for the story: _____
7 Single camera unit; this means that the sound equipment needed is just for one cameraman and reporter with interviewees: _____

e Complete the following definitions using the terms in **bold** in the filming schedule in Exercise 3b.

1 A freelance journalist who sets up interviews and gets permission to film on locations before the crew arrives; also acts as a translator and provides up-to-date information: _____fixer_____
2 Legal documents that interviewees and other contributors to the programme sign to confirm their contributions can be used, usually without receiving any payment: _____
3 An audio recording device: _____
4 This tells the crew how much money they have to spend on food and minor expenses per day: _____
5 This is a tape format like VHS or Beta; it is a high-end filming format, often used by long-format documentaries: _____
6 Digibeta tapes which the camera operator records footage onto: _____
7 A series of filmed shots that can be edited together to form a single section of the documentary: _____
8 Customs documents often needed when taking expensive equipment outside the European Union: _____

f ▶4.3 Donna Eery (*SBC* editor) and Penny Cole (production manager) are checking whether everything is in order prior to their departure to the shoot location. Listen to four excerpts from their conversation and decide which term in the box best describes what they are talking about in each excerpt.

> carnets   daily rates   tape stock   release forms

1 _____
2 _____
3 _____
4 _____

g Complete the rest of *SBC*'s filming schedule below using the verbs in the box. There may be more than one possible answer.

> film   get   IV   R/V   travel

FILMING SCHEDULE

Friday 26 October

10.00	(1) _____ at police headquarters.	
	(2) _____ permission for shooting.	
12.00	(3) _____ man who's taking traffickers to court.	
13.00	(4) _____ GVs on location. IV social worker and victims of trafficking. PTC.	
15.00	(5) _____ representative from *People not Borders* organisation.	

Saturday 27 October

10.30	(6) _____ government official.

TRAVEL DAY

Sunday 28 October

9.00	(7) _____ to airport.
13.00	Departure

---

h In groups, think of a topic you would like to make a documentary about, for example a topic in the news at the moment, or a topic you are knowledgeable or passionate about. Discuss the following points.

- Length of time needed for shooting
- Number of crew members involved and their tasks
- Need for fixers
- Need for GVs

i Write a filming schedule for the documentary discussed in Exercise 3h, using the schedule on page 45 as a model. Include as many details as possible.

Filming on location

4 a **In pairs, discuss the following questions.**

1 Have you ever taken part in a shoot on location? If so, what were you filming and why? If not, what kind of shoot would you like to take part in?
2 If you could have any role in a TV film crew, which role would you have? Explain why.

b ▶4.4 **The *Bird's Eye View* crew are on location at a border crossing point. Listen to the conversation and tick (✓) the things that they discuss.**

☐ The sequence of shots taken
☐ The border guards' change of attitude
☐ The effect of the weather on lighting
☐ The distance from the capital
☐ The place where Neil is going to read his script
☐ Technical problems with the camera

c **Complete the following definitions using the terms in the box.**

> pan   personal mic   POV   pull focus   tilt   tracking shot   walkie-talkie   ~~windshield~~

1 A covering used to protect a microphone from the noise created by the wind: _____windshield_____
2 A shot where the camera is moved horizontally left-to-right or right-to-left: _____
3 Filming with the camera placed on a wheeled carriage going along a railed track (in the conversation in Exercise 4b, James is taking shots from the car while it is moving along the road): _____
4 Where the reporter or presenter walks and talks to the camera at the same time: _____
5 Shot where the camera is moved vertically up or down: _____
6 Shot where the camera is used to represent the viewpoint of a subject (in the conversation in Exercise 4b, James filmed from under a blanket to suggest the point of view of a woman being secretly smuggled across a border): _____
7 Shot where the camera's focus is moved from one point to another: _____
8 A small microphone often used for interviews and PTCs: _____

d In pairs, test your partner on the vocabulary in Exercise 4c by either drawing or miming the word. You cannot talk!

5 a ▶4.4 Listen to the conversation in Exercise 4b again and tick (✓) the phrases that you hear.

Saying what needs to be done	Asking for and making suggestions	Asking someone to do something
We'll need to get the guards to hold the traffic …	… **I think we should** get down to the PTC now.	… **could you** tell the guards what we want to do, please?
We might need to put the big windshield on it.	**What can we do about** this strong wind?	**Would you mind** asking the guards if that's OK?
We'll give it a go and see what the sound's like.	**I think it'd be good to** have you doing a walkie-talkie …	
We still need to get some good shots from the other side of the border.	This light's too bright. **You'd better** use lenses.	
	What do you think?	
	If you have a better idea, please tell us.	

b In pairs, discuss what kind of things you could or need to do in order to improve your English. Use the phrases in **bold** in the table in Exercise 5a to help you.

> We still need to learn that new vocabulary.

> I think we should test each other after class.

c Look at the filming schedule you wrote for Exercise 3i on page 47. In groups of four, choose one day's filming and imagine that you are in the middle of that day; role play a meeting. Student A, you are the editor; ask the crew to summarise what they have done so far today and discuss what still needs to be done. Student B, you are the camera operator; describe the shots you have taken so far today and talk about any potential problems with the afternoon's filming. Student C, you are a reporter and Student D, you are a fixer; make, ask for, and agree to follow suggestions as necessary.

Editing a TV documentary

6 a In pairs, discuss the following question.
- What is the difference between an editor (or chief/head editor) and an output editor?

b Read the email from Donna, the *Bird's Eye View* editor, on page 50 and answer the following questions.
1 Why has Donna sent this email?
2 Who do you think Diana is?
3 How do you think she will feel when she receives this email?

Hi Diana,

My flight has been delayed by five hours so I'm going to be really late getting to you. Can you get on with editing the people-trafficking programme until I arrive? Sorry!

Can you start on the clipping? You've got the **shot list**, haven't you? Start with the tracking shots and then move on to the interviews. It would be nice to **intercut** them with some sequences we shot on leaving the border. There are some cuts, though, which we'll have a look at together when I arrive. Tell the clipspotter to give you a hand with the time codes.

By the way, I like your idea of the reconstruction of someone being trafficked through the border. It makes it really clear to the audience what actually happened.

Regarding the atmosphere, we'll use some sound **effects** but also drones. We can enhance it with some slow mixes. I've already got the **royalty-free compilation CD**, so we won't have to pay for music.

Please tell the other reporter, Sylvana Calpepper, to come to the editing studio. Neil can't make it because he's ill, although he said he'd try and join us later if he's feeling better. Anyway, tell Sylvana she can start first. Get her to **lay down** her voice and then she can go. I know she's expected to do some recordings in Edinburgh this evening. The booth is ready. Neil has prepared a script and an **EDL**.

Sorry to leave you on your own with all this stuff, but as you know, the schedule is really tight.

If you've any doubts, ring me on my work mobile.

I'll be with you tomorrow at the latest.

Thanks,

Donna

C **Complete the following definitions using the words in bold in the email in Exercise 6b.**

1 Sounds/images produced for a programme or film: _____ effects _____
2 To record: _____
3 A CD containing music you do not need to pay the composer to use:
   _____
4 Edit Decision List; it gives an idea of how the editor wants a programme to be edited: _____
5 To edit and mix two concurrent scenes: _____
6 A list of shots that the crew shot on location, with a description and their time code: _____

d **Circle the correct alternative to complete the following sentences.**

1 Donna uses the verb *can* / *could* to ask Diana to do things.
2 Donna also uses *would you* / **the imperative** to give Diana instructions.
3 The tone of the email is **friendly** / **unfriendly** but authoritative.

7 a ▶4.5 **The *SBC* crew have come back from filming on location. Donna Eery and Neil Wax are now finalising the on-location section of the programme for *Bird's Eye View* with the output editor, Diana Myers. Listen to their conversation and answer the following questions.**

1 Is Diana happy with Donna and her team?
2 Why is Neil in a hurry?

b Complete the following definitions using the words in the box from the conversation in Exercise 7a.

clipspotter   time code   reconstruction   booth   script   ~~mix~~

1   Gradual change made by the output editor from one shot to another, so that you can actually see the next shot appearing: _____ mix _____
2   A soundproof boxed room with a microphone: _____
3   A sequence of numbers put on the tape when a cameraman records a shot so that it is easy to find the shots: _____
4   Someone who speaks the language that the interviewees use and is brought in to translate and identify exactly the clips that the reporter wants to use to illustrate the script: _____
5   The narrative spoken by the reporter in the booth: _____
6   A short, filmed representation of events that have already happened (this is used quite often in current affairs programmes, when it is difficult to get actual footage of the events that are being talked about): _____

c ▶4.5 Listen again and match the beginnings (1–6) to the endings (a–f).

1	I started off with some GVs and tracking	a	codes here.
2	I followed your suggestion in your email and intercut it	b	up for you …
		c	my voice now?
3	… it's almost like a reconstruction	d	with some sequences you shot at the border.
4	I've got all the time	e	of someone being trafficked.
5	… can I record	f	shots, then moved on to the interviews you did.
6	The booth's all set		

d In groups, role play an editing session for the documentary you wrote the filming schedule for in Exercise 3i on page 47. Student A, you are the editor; you have overall responsibility for the editing session. Student B, you are the reporter; you need to record the script for the documentary. Student C, you are the output editor; your responsibility is the actual editing (mixing the sound and images). Decide how you will edit your documentary.

e Imagine you are going to be late for a follow-up to the editing session in Exercise 7d. Write an email to your assistant with instructions about what to do. Use the email in Exercise 6b to help you and remember to include the following points:

- Why you are going to be late
- What needs to be done
- What you like about the editing work which has been done so far
- An apology for being late
- Thanks for your assistant's help

- Writing a screenplay
- Pitching successfully
- Organising a shoot
- Writing a film review

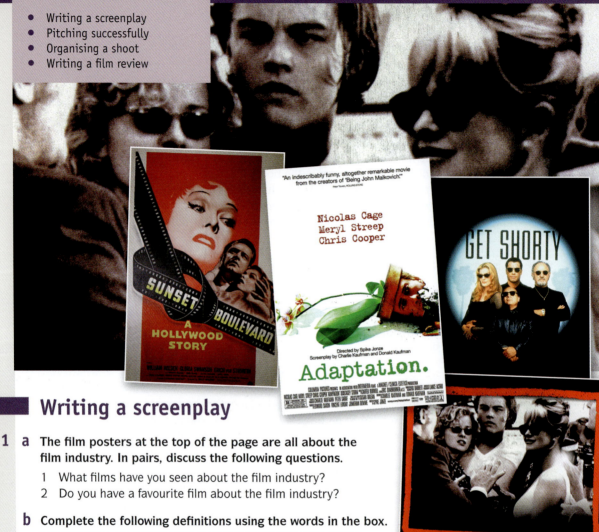

Writing a screenplay

1 a **The film posters at the top of the page are all about the film industry. In pairs, discuss the following questions.**

1 What films have you seen about the film industry?
2 Do you have a favourite film about the film industry?

b **Complete the following definitions using the words in the box.**

> the cast   director   ~~editing~~   plot   screenplay   screenwriter
> special effects   soundtrack   the stars

1 The putting together of sequences and scenes in a film:
   __editing__
2 A story written for a film: _____
3 Someone who writes stories for a film: _____
4 All the actors in a film: _____
5 Series of events in a film that make up the main story: _____
6 Images or sounds in a film that are created by trick photography or computers: _____
7 The music in a film: _____
8 The main actors in a film: _____
9 The person responsible for overall artistic content of film, including telling the cast what to do: _____

c **In pairs, discuss the aspects of a film that are the most important for you when deciding which films to see. Use the words in Exercise 1b to help you.**

2 **a** Most screenplays are divided into three Acts. Match the Acts (1–3) to the descriptions (a–c).

1	Act 1	a	The main conflict
2	Act 2	b	The resolution
3	Act 3	c	The background

b In pairs, think about a film you each know well and take turns to ask and answer the following questions.

1 How is the story set up and how are the characters introduced? (Act 1)
2 What conflict(s) do the characters deal with during the story – that is, what is the problem/desire/goal at the centre of the story? (Act 2)
3 How is/are the conflict(s) resolved at the end of the film? (Act 3)

c Think about a story you would like to tell, or a book you would like to adapt into a film. Make notes under the following headings.

Act 1: The background   Act 2: The conflict   Act 3: The resolution

3 **a** Read a scene from the second draft of the screenplay *Adaptation*, which is about a screenwriter, Kaufman, who is having problems adapting a novel to a screenplay. Answer the following questions.

1 **Who** is involved in the scene?   4 **What** is happening?
2 **Where** does it take place?   5 **Why** is this scene taking place?
3 **When** does it take place?   6 **How** do the protagonists feel?

INT. L.A. BUSINESS LUNCH RESTAURANT – MIDDAY

Kaufman, wearing his purple sweater, sits with Valerie, an attractive woman in glasses. They pick at salads. Kaufman steals glances at her. She looks up at him. He looks away.

KAUFMAN (V.O.)
I'm old. I'm bald. I'm repulsive.

VALERIE
We think you're just great.

KAUFMAN
(with studied modesty)
Oh, thank you.

Valerie rubs her nose. Kaufman self-consciously rubs his nose in response.

VALERIE
And we're thrilled you're interested.

Valerie rubs her nose again. Kaufman pulls at his nostril. Sweat slides down his forehead. Valerie watches it. Kaufman sees her watching it. She sees him seeing her watching it. She looks at her salad. He quickly wipes the sweat away.

KAUFMAN
Oh, thanks, wow. That's nice to hear.

VALERIE
You have a really unique voice.

KAUFMAN
Well, thanks. That's ... I appreciate that.

VALERIE
Very talented. Really.

KAUFMAN
Thanks. Thank you. Thanks.

VALERIE
(looking up)
So –

Kaufman is sweating a lot. He smiles, embarrassed.

KAUFMAN
Sort of hot in here.

VALERIE
(kindly)
Yeah, it is a bit. So, why don't you tell me your thoughts on this crazy little project of ours.

In one motion, Kaufman wipes his forehead and pulls a book entitled The Orchid Thief from his bag.

KAUFMAN
First, I think it's a great book.

VALERIE
Laroche is a fun character, isn't he?

KAUFMAN
It's just, I don't want to compromise by making it a Hollywood product.

VALERIE
Oh, of course. We agree. Definitely.

Kaufman is sweating like crazy now. Valerie is quiet for a moment.

VALERIE
See, we thought maybe Susan Orlean and Laroche could fall in love –

KAUFMAN
New York journalist writes about weird guy and he teaches her to love. I mean, it didn't happen, it wouldn't happen.

INT. OFFICE – DAY

b **In pairs, discuss the following questions.**

1 Do you think Valerie and Kaufman have the same vision for the film?
2 What do you think Kaufman means by "a Hollywood product"?
3 What do you think will happen next?

c **Complete the following statements about the standard format of screenplays, using the words in the box and excerpt in Exercise 3a to help you.**

action   present   centre   V.O.   ~~capital~~   dialogue   INT.   brackets

1 The names of characters and scene headings are written in ___capital___ letters.
2 Dialogue is written in the _____ of the page.
3 Descriptions of settings and _____ are written in blocks which are wider than the dialogue.
4 Descriptions of how a character delivers his lines are in _____ .
5 Characters generally have little _____ at one time.
6 Descriptions of settings and actions are written in the _____ tenses.
7 Voice-overs are abbreviated as _____ , external shots as *EXT.* and internal shots as _____ .

d **Read a later scene from the same screenplay and answer the following question.**

- Who do you think McKee is?

INT. BAR – NIGHT

Kaufman and McKee are sat at a table with beers. Kaufman is reading from his copy of The Orchid Thief.

KAUFMAN
(pause)
I've got pages of false starts. I'm way past my deadline. I can't go back.

MCKEE
Ah, the ever-present deadline. Yes, I was doing a Kojak episode once and … it was hell.

McKee drinks his beer, watching Kaufman.

MCKEE
Tell you a secret. The last act makes the film. You can have a boring movie, but wow them at the end, and you've got a hit. Find an ending. Use what you've learned this weekend. Give them that, and you'll be fine.

Tears form in Kaufman's eyes.

KAUFMAN
You promise?

McKee smiles. Kaufman hugs him.

MCKEE
You've taken my course before?

KAUFMAN
My brother did. My twin brother, Donald. He's the one who got me to come.

MCKEE
Twin screenwriters. Julius and Philip Epstein, who wrote *Casablanca*, were twins.

KAUFMAN
You mentioned that in class.

MCKEE
The finest screenplay ever written.

---

e **In pairs, discuss the following questions.**

1 What do you think of McKee's advice that a "wow" ending can save a bad film?
2 Think of a film ending that you like/dislike. What do you like/dislike about it?
3 What do you think is "the finest screenplay ever written"? Do you agree with McKee's choice?

f Look at the following list of features that are typical of spoken dialogues, with examples from the screenplay in Exercise 3a. Can you find any more examples of these features in the screenplay in Exercise 3d?

Feature	Examples
Incomplete sentences	*That's … I appreciate that.*
Missing subjects	*Sort of hot in here.*
Repetition	*Thanks. Thank you. Thanks.*
Short sentences	*We agree.*
Simple linking words	*So, why don't you tell me your thoughts …*
Use of shared knowledge to leave things unsaid	*We (i.e. the people at the film studio)* think *you're just great.*

g In pairs, make a list of any other features typical of spoken conversations and screenplay dialogues.

Interruptions, rephrasing

h Write a scene for the film you made notes on for Exercise 2c. Use standard screenplay format and make the conversation seem as natural as possible.

Pitching successfully

4 a In pairs, discuss the following questions.

1 Once you have written a screenplay, what do you think is the next step?
2 Which is more important: talent or being in the right place at the right time?

b You are going to read a query letter written by a screenwriter. In pairs, discuss what you think a query letter might be.

c Read the query letter and check your answer to Exercise 4b.

Dear Mr Godfrey,

I have recently completed my second screenplay, entitled *on stAGE*. Last year I completed a one-year postgraduate course in screenwriting at London Metropolitan University, and I was one of the ten finalists in the Nicholl Fellowships in Screenwriting. I would like to ask if you would consider reading my latest work.

on stAGE is a touching musical comedy set in the North of England about a group of men who, on turning 40, decide to re-form their teenage band but find that teenage values and ideas aren't always the same across generations. There are a number of great rock scenes which are accompanied by a wonderful soundtrack of classic songs from the last three decades. *on stAGE* is a feelgood film which combines tears and laughter. Think *Spinal Tap* meets *The Breakfast Club*. I am confident it will generate lots of critical and box office success.

If you are interested in reading my screenplay, please contact me at the address at the top of the page.

Yours sincerely,

Jamie Louis

Jamie Louis

d Read the query letter in Exercise 4c again and decide if the following statements are True (T) or False (F).

1 The first paragraph outlines the writer's credentials and the reason for writing.
2 The second paragraph outlines the plot and the most important points about the screenplay.
3 All the tenses in the second paragraph are either present tenses or the modal verb *might*.
4 The third paragraph says what the reader should do.
5 The letter is quite informal.

e Write a query letter for the film you outlined in Exercise 2c or a film you have seen recently, using the query letter in Exercise 4c to help you.

5 a Read the advert for a seminar and answer the following questions.

1 What is a *pitch*?
2 Do you think the seminar would be interesting and/or useful? Explain why / why not.

FILMMAKING IN THE DIGITAL AGE with Michael Wiese

About the Pitch Session

SEMINAR EMPHASIS: GET THE MONEY!

Background

The Pitch Session is the most popular and challenging part of the seminar. Besides filmmakers, we are inviting investors to the seminar who may be willing to invest millions of dollars if they learn about a project they like. To increase your chances of obtaining the financing and resources you need, we recommend you prepare your pitch before the seminar.

The Pitch Session

Your pitch will be one or two minutes in length.

Key Elements of Your Pitch

Your opening sentences will include:

- The (1) _____ : is it a comedy, a thriller, a drama, a teen movie, a documentary, etc.?
- The (2) _____ : something active and engaging that would make us want to see the film.
- The (3) _____ : a one-sentence synopsis of the screenplay.
- Any other (4) _____ : anything else that will get people's interest (target audience, location, music, etc.).

Practising Your Pitch

Write out the most significant selling points, and then pitch it until it naturally rolls off your tongue and you no longer need notes. The pitch itself will evolve as you practise – you'll quickly find what works and what doesn't.

Stand up and pitch to family and friends; describe your project using the four elements above; use your hands to express yourself; make eye contact with the audience; be aware of your physical appearance and dress appropriately; remember that the most successful people are natural at presenting themselves, so use humour where appropriate and engage authentically in a real one-to-one dialogue with the audience.

b **Read the advert in Exercise 5a again and answer the following questions.**

1 Who do you think Michael Wiese is?
2 Who is the seminar for?
3 Who else might be present?
4 How much time will the people attending the seminar have in order to pitch their film?
5 When will the pitches be prepared?
6 Why are family and friends mentioned?
7 In what other situations do you think the skills involved in pitching would be useful?

c **Complete the advert in Exercise 5a using the words in the box.**

genre   hooks   logline   title

d **Match the film titles (1–3) to the loglines (a–c).**

1	*The Shakespeare Code*	a	This is a story about a group of men who, on turning 40, decide to re-form their teenage band but find that teenage values and ideas aren't always the same across generations.
		b	The story is about Sylvia, who is drawn into a conspiracy encoded in the writings of Shakespeare, only to find that the people she trusts most are those most able to harm her.
2	*Conviction*		
3	*on stAGE*	c	Set in the 1970s, it's a story about an ex-convict-turned-policeman who discovers that a string of brutal NYPD cop killings are part of a larger conspiracy.

e **In pairs, discuss the following questions.**

1 What is the purpose of a *logline*?
2 Why do you think loglines are so important for screenwriters and film executives?

f **Match the formulas for writing loglines (1–3) to an example in Exercise 5d.**

1 ... story about (character), who (problem), only to find that (conflict).
2 ... story about (character) who discovers that (problem and conflict).
3 ... story about (character), who (problem), but finds that (conflict).

g **Write a logline for the film you made notes on for Exercise 2c or for a film you have seen recently. Then, in groups, compare your loglines. Decide which you think are the most effective. Explain your answer.**

6 a ▶5.1 **Listen to a pitch for one of the films in Exercise 5d and answer the following questions.**

1 Which film is being pitched?
2 What hooks (for example, music and location) does the screenwriter mention?
3 If you were a film executive, would you invest money in this film? Explain why / why not.

b ▶5.1 **Listen again and tick (✓) the phrases that you hear.**

Small talk	The pitch	Clarifying information about the pitch	Ending the pitch meeting
I hope you found us without any problem?	My film's called ...	... could you explain how the audience is expected to believe that ... ?	If you leave a copy with us, we'll get back to you within ...
I trust you had no problem getting here?	It's a (touching musical comedy) set in ...	Can you tell me more about ... ?	That's everything for now. We'll be in touch one way or the other.
So, is this your first screenplay?	This film is aimed at ...	I don't fully understand ...	
	There are a number of great ...		
	(on stAGE) is a feelgood film ...		
	Think (*Spinal Tap*) meets (*The Breakfast Club*).		

c **In pairs, role play a pitch. Student A, you are pitching the film you have prepared your logline for in Exercise 5g; Student B, you are a film executive. Student B, you must assess Student A's pitch and give feedback. Use the notes in the box on the right to help you. Swap roles and practise again.**

Name of film:	
Mentions	**Uses**
☐ genre ☐ title ☐ logline ☐ hooks: _____	☐ eye contact ☐ hand gestures ☐ relaxed style
How effective is the pitch? ___/10	

Organising a shoot

7 a **In groups, discuss the following questions.**

1 Have you ever had any experience in film production? If so, what did you do? If not, what would you like to do?
2 What do the following people do during the production of a film?
   ● film producer ● film director ● director of photography ● sound director
3 Of the people above, who do you think is the most important to a film's success?

b ▶5.2 **A pre-production meeting for the film *The Mystery of the Maharashtra Caves* is taking place at Hindi Films Production Bollywood Ltd., in Bombay. Listen to the meeting and tick (✓) the points they discuss.**

☐ Finance
☐ Road conditions
☐ Permission to shoot on certain locations
☐ Availability of electricity on site
☐ Availability of facilities on site
☐ Technical issues
☐ The need to contact a location agency

c Match the terms from the pre-production meeting (1–9) to their meanings (a–i).

1	lighting rig	a	the activity of organising practical and financial matters connected with the preparation of a film
2	reconnoitre (recce)		
3	sound crew	b	coloured glass which controls the light entering a camera
4	production	c	the team taking care of shooting and photography
5	to shoot	d	an organisation providing location management for film production purposes
6	camera crew	e	the team taking care of the sound system
7	generator	f	a machine producing electricity
8	filters	g	to film
9	location agency	h	a check that everything is OK with logistics and technical equipment on location
		i	a system for lighting a location

d ▶5.2 Look at the two alternative words/phrases in *italics* in the table below. In each case, both alternatives are possible, but only one is said in the pre-production meeting. In pairs, try to remember what was said, then listen and check your answers. The extracts are numbered in the order they appear in Audio 5.2.

Explaining potential problems	Presenting solutions
1 ... **there are practically no problems with** access for *teams and equipment / crews and gear* ...	2 **My next recces will be aimed at** checking on *medical care and safety / health and safety* in case anything happens while we're on location ... .
3 ... **my main concern at this stage is that** whatever *locations/sites* we select, we need to bear in mind how they will look on film.	6 ... my camera crew think **the problem can be solved with** *extra lighting rigs / additional lighting equipment* ..., and *filters / lens protectors* that reduce the amount of light let into the camera.
4 ... **we also need to avoid any problems that** may slow down *filming/shooting* ...	7 **I'll try to get** you the *most advanced / most reliable* generators we can.
5 ... **I'm a little concerned about** the *lighting/illumination* ...	8 **I've decided to** contact our usual *location agency / full-service location agency* ...

e The expressions in **bold** in the table above are used for explaining potential problems and solving them. In pairs, practise using the expressions. Student A, read out the expressions in bold; Student B, try to complete the phrase without looking at your book. Swap roles and practise again.

f In groups of four, role play a meeting to discuss shooting on location. Student A, you are the film producer; Student B, you are the film director; Student C, you are the director of photography; and Student D, you are the sound director. Choose a film from the following: one of the film treatments you outlined in Exercise 2c, *on stAGE* in Exercise 5d, or a real film you are all familiar with. The following list includes some possible problems you may have to solve.

* getting local authorities' permission to shoot at certain locations
* no electricity or other facilities available
* testing all the equipment before using it
* needing local actors in crowd scenes
* making sure there is easy access to everywhere we need to shoot
* other?

Writing a film review

8 a In pairs, discuss the following questions.

1 How many different stages are there from the initial idea for a film to the film being shown to a paying audience?
2 Who do you consider to have the most important role in the success of a film: the creative people or the investors, promoters and distributors?

b Put the following stages in the journey from film concept to cinema/DVD screen in the correct order.

☐ Copies are sent to the cinemas a few days before they start showing the film.
☐ The studio or producer decides the number of <u>prints</u> of the film to make.
☐ The buyers make an agreement with the distribution company about which films they wish to <u>lease</u> and fix the terms of the lease agreement (i.e. % of the <u>box office</u>).
☐ A studio or producer buys the <u>rights</u> to the film.
☐ The film is shot, and when completed is sent to the <u>studio</u>.
☐ When the film <u>run</u> ends, the film is returned to the distribution company, which pays the amount due.
5 The studio signs a <u>licensing agreement</u> with a distribution company.
☐ At <u>screenings</u>, the film is shown to potential buyers representing the cinema chains.
☐ A producer, director, cast and camera/sound crew are hired to make the film.
1 A screenwriter has an idea for a film, which is pitched to potential investors.

c Complete the following definitions using the <u>underlined</u> words in Exercise 8b.

1 Legal authority over who may use a film: _____rights_____
2 Place where films are edited and produced: _____
3 Contract giving someone the legal right to use a film: _____
4 Copies of the film: _____
5 Rent: _____
6 Ticket sales; literally, the place where people buy tickets at a cinema: _____
7 Period in which a film is shown: _____
8 Showings of the film: _____

d In pairs, try to describe the stages of a film from concept to screening, without looking back at Exercise 8b. Correct any mistakes in your partner's description.

9 a In groups, discuss the following questions.

1 Do you ever read film reviews? Explain why / why not.
2 How much influence do you think critics have on the amount of money a film makes?
3 Do you think film reviews should be written by people who have been involved in the film industry, by reviewers specialising in film, or by ordinary journalists?

b Read the film review. Would you like to see the film? Explain why / why not.

The Killing of John Lennon Cosmo Landesman

1 This is a **well-researched**, **fact-based** drama about Mark Chapman, the man who, in December 1980, murdered Lennon. Since we know what happened, all that's left for the writer and director, Andrew Piddington, to explore, is the mysterious: Why? And this he does with great enthusiasm, going deep into Chapman's dark, mad mind.

2 The challenge for Piddington is to make the narcissistic nobody Chapman an interesting **character**, which is a result he definitely achieves.

3 But the best thing about the film is that it successfully challenges the Chapman story as it is conventionally told. First of all, we see he was not your typical isolated, rootless young man. He was not abused as a child or tormented as an adult. Secondly, since killing Lennon he has come to symbolise the dark side of modern celebrity: the fan who becomes the fanatic, who will kill for his own 15 minutes of fame. Yet though Chapman came to enjoy his notoriety, that was not his prime motive; he killed Lennon because he thought he was a hypocrite.

4 What's missing, however, is a sense of the private Chapman. Although we hear a **voice-over** of his actual words, you never really get a sense of him **off camera**, as it were. So we never really get to understand him.

5 The film ends with a curious irony. Chapman must remain in solitary imprisonment forever, to protect him from the peace-loving Lennon fans who want him dead.

Cert 15, 110 mins

☆ ☆ ☆ ☆ ☆

c Read the review again and answer the following questions.

1 Is the review positive or negative?
2 What do the stars at the end stand for?
3 What does *Cert 15* stand for?

d Complete the following definitions using the words in bold in the review.

1 Based on authentic information: _____
2 Not being filmed: _____
3 Carefully investigated: _____
4 Comments of an unseen speaker: _____
5 A person in a film: _____

e Language devices such as connectors can help you write a more coherent and logical text. Match the highlighted connectors in the review to their functions (1–4). If you can, add more connectors to each function.

1 To give contrasting information
2 To give additional information
3 To order points
4 To show cause and effect

f Complete a different review of *The Killing of John Lennon*, taken from a newspaper, using the connectors in Exercise 9e.

Here is the film that many people, especially Lennon's fans, have been waiting for all these years. A homage to the great Lennon, different in tone from similar films.

(1) _____ he was killed 18 years ago, our interest in John Lennon continues to this day. (2) _____ Andrew Piddington's new film, The Killing of John Lennon, taps into our collective fascination in two novel ways: (3) _____ , by presenting a new side to Lennon's killer, Mark Chapman; (4) _____ , by drawing parallels between Chapman's actions and our current fascination with celebrity.

(5) _____ the story of Lennon's murder is so well known, it is to Piddington's credit that the film is both gripping and (6) _____ revelatory. Highly recommended.

The Killing of John Lennon
★★★★★

g Match the paragraph numbers in the film review in Exercise 9b (1–5) to their functions (a–e).

a Tells us what is bad about the film
b Introduces the film: genre, director, basic plot
c Concludes the review in an interesting way
d Tells us what is difficult for the film to do and whether it achieves it
e Tells us what is good about the film

h Match the phrases (1–5) to the functions in Exercise 9g (a–e).

1 The best thing about the film is …
2 The film ends with …
3 This is a well-researched, fact-based drama about …
4 What's missing, however, is …
5 The challenge for the director is to …

i Think of a film you have recently seen. In pairs, take turns to say what you thought about the film, using the phrases in Exercise 9h.

10 **a** Does the review in Exercise 9b meet the following requirements of a good film review (1–5)? Explain why / why not.

1 It is written using mostly the present tense.
2 It gives a brief outline of the plot and characters without revealing everything, so that readers will want to see the film to know how it develops and ends.
3 It avoids using over-emphatic language such as *the best film ever* and *superb acting*.
4 It provides a critical assessment of the successes/failings of the film, based on a specific example from the film.
5 It highlights features, when relevant, which make the film worth seeing.

b You are going to write a review of the film you talked about in Exercise 9i. Before you write your review, answer the following questions.

1 Is the film a novel/play adaptation? How close is it to the original? Is its cinematographic version better or worse than the novel itself?
2 Alternatively, is the film based on an original screenplay? Is it new and fresh?
3 Are the characters convincing?
4 Is the casting up to your expectations?
5 Is the theme of the film successfully conveyed to the audience?
6 Is the setting appropriate and effective?
7 Are camera effects (texture, lighting, colour, etc.) and the soundtrack effective and functional? Do they enhance the mood, theme and setting of the film?

c Make notes for your review under the headings in Exercise 9g.

d Write your review. Add connectors to make it clearer to read. When you have finished, read your review and correct any mistakes.

e Read as many of your classmates' reviews as possible. Decide which you think is the best review and which film you would most like to see.

UNIT 6 New media

- Briefing a website designer
- Analysing problems and providing solutions
- Planning and writing a blog
- Creating a podcast

Briefing a website designer

1 a **In groups, discuss the following questions.**

1 Do you think you are web-savvy – that is, do you have a good understanding of the Internet? Explain why / why not.
2 When was the last time you went online? What for?
3 Describe your favourite website or a website that you often visit.
4 Do you ever buy things online? Explain why / why not.

b Label the home page of *The Scottish Bookshop* using the words in the box.

> drop-down menu   search function   shopping cart/basket   hyperlink
> sidebar   ~~domain name~~

1 _domain name_

2 _____

www.thescottishbookshop.com

Looking for a book? *You can search by Author, Title or ISBN*
Search (_____)

6 _____

The Scottish Bookshop

Home | My Account | Check out | Contact Us

New releases!
See our newest stock!
New release books

BOOK CATEGORIES

Scottish Fiction
Scottish Subjects
Scottish Children's Books
Audio Books
Gift Suggestions

BOOKSHOP INFORMATION

About Us

Delivery Rates

Finding Books

Welcome to the Scottish Bookshop!

Welcome to the Scottish Bookshop. We hope you find it a good place to shop. You can put books in a shopping basket and order a number of books at once.

Most books have a 15% discount!

Click **here** for more information.

5 _____

You can order any book that is in print, whether it is listed or not. If you want a book that is not listed, send the details to Gavin Bennett (gavin_bennett@thescottishbookshop.com).

Your Cart Total
0 items
Total £0.00

Customer login

Email: ( )

Password: ( )

Forgotten your password?

Log in

© 2008
The Scottish Bookshop

Privacy Policy

Site Map

4 _____

3 _____

c In pairs, practise saying aloud:

1 the website address
2 Gavin's email address.

d ▶6.1 **Listen and check your answers.**

e In pairs, swap your email address and favourite website addresses by saying them aloud.

2 **a** ▶6.2 *The Scottish Bookshop* owners are discussing the construction of their website with a freelance web designer. Listen to three extracts from their meeting and tick (✓) the points that they discuss.

☐ *The Scottish Bookshop*'s needs and objectives
☐ Time schedule for construction of website
☐ Price
☐ Features of the website

b Listen again and decide if the following statements are True (T) or False (F).

1 Ian knows a lot about the Internet.   F
2 Ian and Fiona think it's very important to sell books online.
3 They can't use the domain name www.thescottishbookshop.com.
4 They will be responsible for running the server.
5 If they include a lot of images on the website, it will run more slowly.
6 Their son, Gareth, will be able to maintain the site.

c ▶6.2 **Complete the phrases from Audio 6.2 in the following table. Then check your answers using the audioscript on page 97.**

Asking for definitions	Giving definitions	Bringing a meeting to a close
Domain ____*what*____ , sorry? ____*What's*____ that?	A web hosting service is a _____ of service which ...	It's been really interesting _____ to you.
What _____ are web hosting services?	A server is a _____ of computer system which ...	I look forward to doing _____ with you.
		Thanks for _____ here today.

d Complete the table in Exercise 2b by writing the following phrases in the correct column.

1 Its function is ...
2 I think we've covered everything.
3 What do you mean when you say "..." ?
4 It's used for ...
5 It means ...
6 You use it to ...
7 It's like a ...

e In pairs, look back at the vocabulary in Exercise 1b. Take turns to define words using the expressions in the table in Exercise 2b.

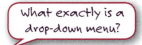

What exactly is a drop-down menu?

Well, it's used for ...

f Complete the following extracts from the meeting in Exercise 2a using the words in the box.

> if 'll (x2) once so the (x2)

1 Neither of us are particularly web-savvy, _____ you'll have to keep your explanations simple.
2 _____ more images you included, _____ slower the download time was, ...
3 _____ you include all these features, you _____ need someone to do web maintenance …
4 _____ he understands the system, he _____ be able to take care of these responsibilities.

g Answer the following questions about the sentences in Exercise 2e.

1 Do all the extracts show a link between cause and effect?
2 Are the two clauses in the phrase *the …* , *the …* followed by comparatives or superlatives?
3 What word is *'ll* a contraction of?
4 Which tenses are used in the sentences beginning with *if* and *once*?
5 Do you know any other time markers that are also followed by a present tense when they refer to the future (for example, *after*)?

h Look at *The Scottish Bookshop*'s website in Exercise 1b again and answer the following questions.

1 Are most of the menu and links complete sentences or noun phrases?
2 What are the two principal categories on the side bar?
3 What information is included in the welcome paragraph?
4 How many lines are there in each paragraph? Why is this?
5 What pronouns are used in the paragraphs to make them seem like a direct dialogue with potential customers?
6 The sentences are either short and simple or are linked by simple words, for example *and/if*. Why do you think this is?
7 Is it possible to contact *The Scottish Bookshop*?
8 Do you think this is a successful home page? Why / why not?

i In groups, design a home page for one of the following: your company, the place where you study English, this book, or your home town.

Analysing problems and providing solutions

3 a **In pairs, discuss the following questions.**

1 What do you understand by the term *new media*?
2 What types of new media are you familiar with? How useful do you find them?

b **In pairs, decide if the following are examples of new or old media. Explain why.**

> books   blogs   multimedia CD-ROMs   cinema   email and attachments
> game consoles   interactive kiosks   interactive television   magazines
> mobile phones   newspapers   podcasts   radio   software   television
> websites   wikis

c **In pairs, decide which examples of new media in Exercise 3b you associate with the following words.**

> broadband connection   free downloads   high definition   video on demand

4 a **A software development consultancy, *Future Solutions*, has written a project vision statement for its client, the digital television provider *The Laughter Network*. Read the project vision statement on page 67. Then choose the correct ending (a, b or c) for the following statements.**

1 The Problem Statement section outlines:
  a the service/product that the client wants.
  b the background of the client's company.
  c both of the above.
2 The Project Vision and Scope section outlines:
  a an overview of *Future Solutions'* background.
  b the solution for the client's needs.
  c both of the above.

b **Read the project vision statement again and answer the following questions.**

1 What does *The Laughter Network* provide?
2 What does *Laughter Network* want to achieve by contracting *Future Solutions*?
3 How does *Future Solutions* suggest meeting *The Laughter Network*'s needs?
4 Why were interactive television applications not successful in the past?
5 What advantages over earlier interactive television applications does the *Future Solutions* project have?
6 Which media are mentioned?

c **In pairs, discuss the following questions.**

1 Do you have to read or write project vision documents or similar documents in your job?
2 The project vision document talks about *social networking*. What other examples of social networking can you think of?

Problem Statement

The Laughter Network has been offering premium satellite and digital television programming for over ten years and has over one million subscribers in the UK.

It has a reputation as a technology leader in the television industry and is always looking for the most **innovative** ways to reach its customers. It was the first channel to offer video on demand, the first to offer a high definition service and the first to sell programmes through a download service.

The Laughter Network wants to extend its customer base into lucrative European markets. In order to achieve this, the product needs to be localised – that is, its content must be either re-dubbed or subtitled into the target market's language. The download service must also be modified to allow payment in different European currencies.

The Laughter Network also wants to create an opportunity to communicate directly with its subscribers and non-subscribers in a direct, social manner.

Project Vision and Scope

The project will see the establishment of a content management application that will manage the process of localising content, by being either re-dubbed or subtitled. To maintain the high quality of the content, a regional web farm will be set up to host the content; this will allow us to use more than one server and deal with large amounts of traffic. The content management application will manage the distribution of the translated content to the appropriate web farm.

In addition, an interactive television application using **cutting-edge** technology will be developed that will combine the **powerful** convergence between television and broadband internet connection with the reach and community provided by a social networking application. This **dynamic** technology platform will permit customers to view *The Laughter Network* content on computers, game consoles and mobile phones, and browse video content with their television remote controls, mouse or keyboard.

The interactive television application will support multiple European payment currencies and will use a payment gateway service that supports these currencies.

Earlier interactive television applications which used previous-generation technology were difficult to build and delivered poor visual quality or had navigation problems. Our solution, using the latest tools and technology, will guarantee an **exceptional** user experience and high-quality presentation.

Users will be able to comment on and discuss programmes with other users, using the interactive television application. The content producers can discuss comments directly with the users, creating a social network where users become more engaged with *The Laughter Network*.

future solutions

d Look at the project vision statement again and decide if the following statements are True (T) or False (F).

1 It is an informal business document.
2 There are no contractions.
3 Hardly any specific people are mentioned in the document.
4 The problem statement uses the verb *would like* to indicate what the client wants to achieve.
5 The most commonly used verb form in the project vision section is *will*.

e Look at the words in **bold** in the project vision statement and answer the following questions by (circling) the correct alternative.

1 They are all **adjectives/adverbs**.
2 They are used to make the writing **more/less** descriptive.
3 The word *innovative* is used in its **comparative/superlative** form to give it more emphasis.

f Complete the following extract from another project vision statement using the adjectives in the box.

> interactive   engaging   extensive   ~~renowned~~   the latest   detailed

The (1) _renowned_ Montreal Huskies hockey team needs to engage and interact with fans over the Internet, and to use that relationship to increase revenue. However, the team's current website is ineffective. The Huskies will use (2) _____ software to build an (3) _____ social networking site, through which the team will be able to provide a fast, (4) _____ and reliable fan experience. The new site will also include the ability to collect (5) _____ fan profile data, create (6) _____ reports, and integrate with sponsors' websites. This solution will be easy to use and cost-effective.

g Look at the following phrases from the project vision document on page 67 and decide whether they are from the Problem Statement (PS) or the Project Vision and Scope (PVS).

1 It has a reputation as … PS
2 Our solution will guarantee …
3 The project will see the establishment of …
4 (*The Laughter Network*) wants to create an opportunity to …
5 It will combine the powerful convergence between …
6 This dynamic technology platform will permit …

h Look at the following notes, written by an employee of *Future Solutions*, about another client, *Weather Wise*, and then complete the sentences (1–4).

> <u>The company</u>: *Weather Wise* provides broadband and wireless weather forecasts and produces the *Weather Wise* website. It is one of the leading providers of weather news.
>
> <u>The problem</u>: *Weather Wise* staff (weather experts, editors, producers) do not have a central location to store documents and collaborate on projects. This makes it difficult for staff to find information.
>
> <u>The solution</u>: A collaborative portal (Intranet) which provides a single tool for information search, supports team collaboration and encourages increased search usage. It can be accessed easily. This will increase staff efficiency and make management decisions faster.

1 *Weather Wise* has a reputation as …
2 *Weather Wise* wants to create an opportunity …
3 The project will see the establishment of …
4 Our solution will guarantee …

i Imagine you work for *Future Solutions*. Write a project vision document for *Weather Wise*. Use the notes in Exercise 4h and the other points in this section to help you. Remember to add adjectives to make the project and solution sound more exciting.

Planning and writing a blog

5 a In pairs, discuss the following questions.

1 Do you ever read blogs? What is the difference between a blog and a website?
2 Is blogging popular in your country?
3 Do you think blogs will ever take over from traditional journalism?
4 What makes a good blog?

b Look at the home page of the website *Notes from Spain* and discuss the following questions.

1 Do you think the site looks interesting?
2 What kind of information do you think is included on the site?

C Look at the following blog entry by Ben, who runs *Notes from Spain*. Put the paragraphs in Ben's blog (A–E) in the correct order.

1 ___D___ 2 _____ 3 _____ 4 _____ 5 _____

http://www.notesfromspain.com/2007/07/31/notes-from-spain-the-story-so-far/

Notes from Spain
Travel - Life - Culture

Home   Forum   Podcasts   Book   Learn Spanish   About   Contact   Faq

Explore Spain:
- Spain Podcasts
- Travel in Spain
- Spanish Music
- Food/Drink
- Food Podcasts
- Living in Spain
- Working in Spain
- Books and Film
- Spain Photos
- Spain Video

Useful Resources:
- Learn Spanish
- Cool Spanish
- Book Review
- Madrid Guide
- Posts

RSS:
🔊 Blog RSS
iTunes NFS in iTunes

Notes from Spain – the story so far…

by Ben Curtis

A So that's basically my story. Hey, Spain bloggers, lovers and visitors – tell us one of your stories!

B This blog started life as an experiment. I wanted to know how blogs worked, so I posted the odd picture from Madrid, or comment on a Spanish news item, etc. At about the same time I wrote an article for *In Madrid,* the local English language rag, on technology, which led to adding the *Notes from Spain* podcasts to this blog – at first on my own, then Marina got involved. We started by making a travel cast, then a cooking cast, and the podcasts started to improve.

C Then I was contacted by a commissioning editor at *Fodors* who had enjoyed the podcasts and wanted me to edit a chapter for their 2007 Spain guide. I chose Galicia and Asturias, and Marina and I spent a couple of weeks in the north of Spain doing research. This year I wrote a couple of introductory sections for their 2008 guide. Wow, *Lonely Planet* and *Fodors*, and all because of the podcasts!

D After returning home from a recent trip to Thailand I found that I had blogger's block. I couldn't think of anything to write about connected with Spain. Then I read a great piece of advice on another site. The piece of advice was to use a blog post to tell a story, so here goes. A question I am occasionally asked about my book, *Errant in Iberia,* is "what happened next", and this is part of the story.

E Now the interesting bit. The *Notes from Spain* podcasts have led to wonderful things. First of all, work with *Lonely Planet*. A few years ago, I wrote several emails to the person in charge of online content, complaining that the first *Lonely Planet* podcasts were boring and that they should produce shows like the ones we were putting together on our trips around Spain. Eventually, after my third email, a very nice man called John got back to me, and purchased one of our podcasts for their feed. We have now made five podcasts for *Lonely Planet*. When I stop to think about it, making podcasts for *Lonely Planet* is a dream come true. It was the first time I had ever had the guts to repeatedly contact an institution I admired, and it really paid off!

Site search

Our Projects…

Free Report   Forget Everything You Know About Learning Spanish

● *Notes in Spanish*

Recent Comments
bill on **Books Rise in Spain as Subtitles Appear on TV!**

Tom on **Books Rise in Spain as Subtitles Appear on TV!**

Pepino on **Books Rise in Spain as Subtitles Appear on TV!**

Recent Posts
Conversation Starters in Spanish
Spanish Divorcees and New TV
Don't Move to a Better Life in Spain

Archives
June 2008
May 2008
April 2008
March 2008
February 2008
January 2008
December 2007
November 2007
October 2007
September 2007
August 2007
July 2007
June 2007
May 2007

d Words in English can have more than one meaning. Look at the dictionary entries for *block* and *post*. Which definition corresponds to the meaning of the words as they are used in Ben's blog?

> **block** (*noun*)
> **1** something that stops (mental) activity
> **2** unit of data in computing

> **post** (*verb*)
> **1** the act of sending a letter or parcel by postal service
> **2** to publish something online

e Choose the correct definition (a or b) for the following highlighted words from Ben's blog.

1	**odd**	a	strange	(b)	occasional
2	**rag**	a	piece of cloth	b	magazine
3	**cast**	a	broadcast	b	the actors in a film
4	**couple**	a	two	b	two people in a relationship
5	**feed**	a	food for animals	b	updated content link
6	**guts**	a	courage	b	intestines
7	**paid off**	a	paid back money	b	brought good results

f Complete the following statements about Ben's blog by (circling) the correct alternative.

1 He speaks to his audience as if they (**are**) / **are not** friends.
2 He uses the first person pronouns *I* and *we* **a lot** / **a little**.
3 He **uses** / **doesn't use** interjections like *hey* and *wow*.
4 He **uses** / **doesn't use** dashes (–) and exclamation marks (!).
5 He **joins** / **doesn't join** sentences with *and* rather than *moreover*, *however* and *therefore*.
6 He uses **some/no** slang words.
7 He **rarely/usually** uses contractions.
8 As a result of the above points, his style is **formal/informal**.

g Complete the following tips for successful blogging, using the words in the box.

> knowledgeable   main   mistakes   ~~entries~~   titles   useful   white space

1 Readers only have a short attention span so keep your blog ___entries___ short.
2 Blogs must be _____ ; for example, they should provide the reader with entertainment, news, debate, etc.
3 Use short, descriptive, interesting _____ for blog entries.
4 Use headings, sub-headings, lists, _____ , photos, images, underlining, etc. to help readers navigate your blog more quickly.
5 Blog about something you are _____ or passionate about.
6 Include your _____ point in the first couple of sentences so readers can decide if they want to continue reading your post.
7 Check your blog for _____ . A well-written blog is easier to read than a blog with confused content and language errors.

h In pairs, discuss whether you agree with statements 1–7 above.

i In pairs, discuss what kind of blog you would write. Explain why.

j Write a brief entry for the blog you talked about in Exercise 5i. Use the guidelines in Exercise 5g to help you.

Creating a podcast

6 a In pairs, discuss the following questions.

1 Have you ever made or listened to a podcast?
2 What makes a good podcast?

b In one of their *Notes from Spain* podcasts, Ben and Marina talk about the financial and legal sides of setting up their website. In pairs, make a list of the possible points they might mention.

Financial matters: *processing payments*   Legal matters:

c ▶6.3 Listen to the podcast and check your answers.

d ▶6.3 Listen again and complete the following extracts.

1 ... my dad, who is 65, is buying a lot on the Internet. _____ , problem number one is that you will probably have to find an accountant who ...
2 ... in a way that he could understand. _____ , the other problem is that the accountant is going to have to work with you and a lawyer to ...
3 ... as most of our customer base is English-speaking. _____ , what's next? Setting up your website.

e Decide if the following statements are True (T) or False (F).

1 Words such as *now*, *so* and *OK* are used in the podcast to move the conversation forward.
2 Words such as *now*, *so* and *OK* are used in the podcast to show agreement.

f ▶6.4 In the second part of the podcast, Ben and Marina discuss setting up the actual website and sources of inspiration. Listen and tick (✓) the points that they discuss.

Setting up the website:
- ☐ Host company
- ☐ Bandwidth
- ☐ Software
- ☐ Hardware
- ☐ Web design

Inspiration:
- ☐ Books
- ☐ Websites
- ☐ People

g ▶6.4 Listen again and complete the following extracts using the words in the box.

actually	~~cos~~	er	OK	so	wait	right	yeah

1 Well, the main reason our web host is in the USA is ___cos___ it's cheaper.
2 ... on their server. _____ , let's move on to talk about getting your website designed.
3 ... all around the world ... _____ . That's E-L-A-N-C-E dot com, *elance.com*. Very useful.
4 We _____ did all of the web design ourselves, using Open Source software.
5 ... is free. _____ , I think that's most of the main points covered. _____ , finally, how about if people want a bit of inspiration?
6 OK, _____ , I think that's at fourhourworkweek.com or ...

h The words and phrases in the box in Exercise 6g are typical of spoken English. Match the words in the box to the descriptions of how they are used (1–7). Some of the words may be used in more than one way.

1 to move conversation forward OK, right
2 another way of saying *yes*
3 an abbreviation of *because*
4 to emphasise a point
5 a sound people make when they are thinking what to say
6 to interrupt someone
7 to get someone's attention before you say something

i Words that are often used together are called collocations. There were several collocations in the podcast, for example *set up a website*. Using correct collocations can make your English sound more natural. Complete the word webs using the nouns in the box. Some of the verbs and nouns may collocate in more than one way.

an agreement a business a client a company a contract
guidelines the main points a proposal a website

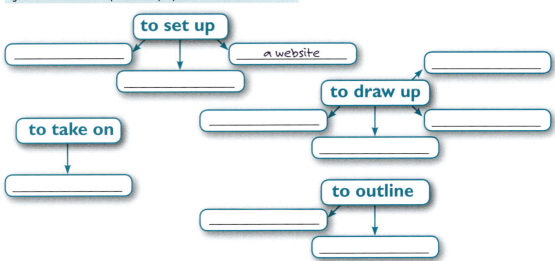

7 a Plan a podcast based on the topic of the blog you wrote about for Exercise 5j. Make notes about three things you will talk about in your podcast.

b Work in pairs and act out or record your podcast. Use the following expressions to help you.

Starting a podcast
Hello, and welcome to the latest podcast from …
Today we're going to be talking about …
Hello, everyone. It's [your name] here with another episode of [title of podcast].

Moving conversation forward
Let's move on to talk about …
OK, what's next?
Now, …
So, …

Ending a podcast
Well, that's all for now.
Links to everything as usual over at [your website].
We'll see you soon. Find us at [your website].
Well, that's it for now from [title of podcast].
So, I hope you've enjoyed this podcast. This is [your name] signing off. Until next time.

- Selling your services to a potential client
- Creating a print advert
- Creating a screen advert
- Presenting a finished advert

Selling your services to a potential client

1 **a** **In pairs, discuss the following questions.**

1 Do you work in advertising? If so, describe your job. If not, what do you think are the good and bad points of working in the advertising industry?
2 What role do advertising agencies play in a successful advertising campaign?
3 Do you think smaller advertising agencies can compete with and be as successful as larger ones? Explain why / why not.

b ▶**7.1** **Some colleagues from an advertising agency, *Media Design Advertising*, are meeting with representatives of a prospective client, *The Daily Sunshine* newspaper. Listen to the meeting and complete the missing information in the notes below. Which two pieces of information are not mentioned?**

Media Design Advertising   Headquarters: _____

Date of meeting: *22 July, 2008*   **Place of meeting:** _____

Client: *The Daily Sunshine*

Attendants:

Name	Position
Marianne Reed	*managing director*
Raffaella Livingstone	_____
Cecily Valley	_____
Dave Terry	_____
John McEwans	_____
Frances Lohan	_____

Target market: _____
Possible ad types: _____
Budget: _____
Next meeting: _____

c ▶7.1 Listen again and (circle) the words/phrases that you hear.

Selling your company
1 We're a very *long-standing* / (*well-established*) company with many years of valuable experience.
2 We've worked with *lots of* / *many of* the top names ...
3 ... we specialise in *media* / *financial* products.
4 ... we've won *numerous* / *many* awards for our innovative approach to advertising.
5 ... we've never had a dissatisfied *client* / *customer*.
6 I'd like to *begin* / *start* by showing you a few of the campaigns we've produced in the past couple of years ...

Expressing opinions and making comments
7 ... your work is of an extremely high *quality* / *standard*.
8 ... you definitely live up to your *good* / *excellent* reputation.
9 ... those TV ads ... are really *striking* / *impressive*.
10 ... the graphics are incredibly *good* / *effective* ...

d Add any more words that you think could be used in the phrases in the tables in Exercise 1c.

long-standing / well-established / reputable

e ▶7.2 The managing director and general account manager of *Media Design Advertising* are at the follow-up meeting with the brand manager of *The Daily Sunshine*. Listen to the conversation. Do you think *Media Design Advertising* will be able to produce the campaign in time? Explain why / why not.

f ▶7.2 Listen again and complete the following sentences.

Reassuring your clients
1 ... we'll ____make____ ____sure____ you won't regret it.
2 ... I think that we'll _____ _____ _____ do it in three to four months.
3 Realistically, I'_____ _____ four months.
4 ... we won't take _____ than _____ .
5 ... I'll send an _____ tomorrow ...
6 ... we'll provide you with work of an extremely _____ _____ , and make sure you get an _____ campaign.
7 ... you'll have the opportunity to get your adverts trialled with test audiences _____ _____ _____ us.

g In pairs, role play a meeting between an advertising agency and a prospective client. Student A, you work for an advertising agency. Present your agency to the client, Student B. Find out about the product and convince Student B that you are the best agency for the job.
Student B, you are a potential client. You want to advertise a product (a perfume, a car or a telephone company). You want the best service possible. Make sure you discuss and take notes on:
- budget
- deadlines
- any guarantees that are offered.

Swap roles and practise again. Use the language in Exercises 1c and 1f to help you.

2 a Look at the contact report on page 76, which was emailed to *The Daily Sunshine*, and answer the following questions.

1 Who has written the contact report?
2 Who is the contact report for?
3 What is the purpose of the contact report?

Media Design Advertising

Headquarters: Milan, Italy

9802 3rd Avenue
Brooklyn
New York 11367
Tel: 001-718-238-5867
Fax: 001-718-238-1856
Email: r.livingstone@mda.org

Mr J McEwans
The Daily Sunshine
Stony Brook
NY 11749
Tel: 001-631-632-5020
Fax: 001-631-632-2527
Email: JMcE@ds.org

Our Ref: RL/MDA
Your Ref: DS/JMc

August 2, 2008

Dear Mr McEwans

Please find below a (1) __summary__ of the points discussed during yesterday's meeting, and a reply to the brief you sent us for a (2) _____ for your newspaper, *The Daily Sunshine*.

OBJECTIVE
Introduce our company, set a (3) _____ , and decide on campaign style and strategy.

TERMS OF CONTRACT
We agreed to accept the $900,000 budget. One third of this amount will be invested in a (4) _____ campaign and the rest in a (5) _____ TV campaign.

We are pleased to confirm we can meet the (6) _____ of six months from today.

You are entitled to trial our (7) _____ in advance. If, for any (8) _____ , you are not satisfied, you may rescind the contract.

If you have any (9) _____ , please do not hesitate to get back to me.

Yours sincerely

Raffaella Livingstone

Raffaella Livingstone
General Account Manager
Media Design Advertising

---

b Complete the contact report using the words in the box.

campaign	prime-time	reason	adverts	~~summary~~	budget	print	queries	deadline

c Look at the contact report again and answer the following questions.

1 What opening and ending salutations are used?
2 What punctuation follows them?
3 What goes in the top left and top right corners?
4 Where is the date written?
5 Does this contact report, which is sent as an email attachment, follow the same layout as a formal letter?

d Read the contact report again and <u>underline</u> any useful phrases that you could use if you had to write a contact report.

e Write a contact report based on the role play in Exercise 1g, using the contact report in Exercise 2a as a model.

Creating a print advert

3 a In groups, discuss the following questions.

1 Do you often read/see ads in English? Do you unders[...] why / why not.
2 Have you ever produced an ad in your own language[...]
3 What do you think of the standard of ads in your co[...] be improved?
4 Have ads changed in the past few years in general[...]

b In pairs, look at the ads below and discuss the foll[...]

1 Which of these ads get your interest and grab yo[...]
2 What are they advertising?
3 Which ad do you think is the most effective? Wh[...]

IT'S A COMPLICATED PLACE. BUT EASY TO SUBSCRIBE TO.

Subscribe for 3 months and save 62% off the cover price.
Call **800 780 040** quoting ref CPIT, or visit **iht.com/comp5**

International Herald Tribune

BECAUSE YOU HAVE TO KNOW

Seven-day delivery of The Times assures you that you won't miss a day's worth of news, analysis, opportunities that can change your life.

50% OFF home delivery of The New York Times for the first **12 WEEKS** when you pay by credit card.

Call today: **1-800-NYTIMES** (800-698-4637), and mention code 0037Q, or visit **NYTimes.com/savings**.

expect the world®
The New York Times
nytimes.com

This introductory offer is valid only in areas served by The New York Times Delivery Service and to readers who have not had home delivery of The New York Times within the past 90 days. At the end of the introductory period, service will continue at our regular low rate for home delivery unless you cancel your subscription. Your credit card will automatically be charged for each 4-week billing period. For non-credit card subscribers, our regular promotion rate of 50% off for the first 8 weeks applies. Offer expires December 31, 2005.

New York Times

c In pairs, answer the following questions.

1 In the *New York Times* ad, what exactly do you 'have to know'? Think of two different answers.
2 What 'complicated place' is the *International Herald Tribune* ad referring to?
3 The *New York Times* and *International Herald Tribune* ads both have a similar approach. What do you think it is?

4 **a** **In pairs, discuss the following questions.**

1   Did the slogans in the ads on page 77 make you want to read the rest of the text? Explain why / why not.

2   Which do you think are more effective: ads with longer slogans or ads with very short, one-sentence slogans?

b **Complete the following table using the products and brand names in the boxes.**

Product
tour operator   beer   ~~newspaper~~
vermouth (alcoholic drink)   coach company
chocolate   bank   magazine

Brand name
~~The Independent~~   Greyhound USA
Cinzano   Thomas Cook   Barclays   Mars
TIME   Miller

Slogan	Product	Brand name
1 It is, are you?	newspaper	The Independent
2 Go faster. Go for less.		
3 Vibrant, rich, and extremely well-balanced.		
4 Don't just book it, Thomas Cook it.		
5 Getting to the very top with the very best.		
6 A Mars a day helps you work, rest and play.		
7 Get TIME, ahead of time.		
8 The champagne of bottled beer.		

c **Look at the slogans in Exercise 4b again and answer the following questions.**

1   Which slogans contain no nouns?

2   Which types of word are used to communicate most of the meaning instead?

d **Slogans use a variety of language devices. Complete the first column of the table using the language devices in the box. Then write the numbers corresponding to the examples in Exercise 4b in the third column of the table.**

personal pronouns   comparisons   ~~alliteration~~   word play   emphatic language
metaphor   rhyme   repetition

Language device	Definition	Example from Exercise 4b
1 alliteration	The use of the same sound or sounds, especially consonants, at the beginning of several words that are close together	8
2	The use of the same word more than once	
3	The use of strong words to show importance	
4	Playing with words which have more than one meaning (Note: In the example given here, we are reminded of the everyday meaning of the brand name.)	
5	Words used to replace nouns. Words such as *you*, *we* and *us* suggest the audience's identification with the product, or having a certain experience through buying the product.	
6	Repetition of the final sound of a word	
7	An expression that describes someone or something by referring to something else that is considered to possess similar characteristics.	
8	Comparing two things (Note: In advertising, the second term of comparison is hardly ever stated; it is left to the audience to decide.)	

e In advertising slogans, adjectives and verbs are generally used much more frequently than nouns. What do you think are the most common adjectives and verbs used in advertising? Make a list of at least five, and then look at the list on page 108 to compare your answers. Are there any surprising words on the list?

f Using the list on page 108, try to complete the following advertising slogans. There may be more than one possible answer. Then identify what language devices from Exercise 4d are used in each slogan.

1 The Music We All _____Love_____ (*Virgin Radio*, radio station)
   personal pronouns
2 Gillette – The Best a Man Can _____ (*Gillette* razors)
3 Dreams are _____ . Realities are _____ . (*Citi* Bank)
4 Nokia N series. See _____ . Hear _____ . Feel _____ .
   (*Nokia* telephones)
5 The _____ bed on earth is not on earth (*Iberia* airline)
6 _____ a step in your career (*SDA Bocconi University*)
7 You and us. Because global capabilities really are a _____ deal
   (*UBS* Investment Bank)

g Think of a product you love (an MP3 player, a computer, a motorbike, etc.). Imagine you are going to advertise the product in a magazine or newspaper. Decide what three adjectives and verbs you would use to describe it.

h In groups, choose one of the products in Exercise 4g and write a print ad for it. Use some of the language devices you have studied in this section to help you.

Creating a screen advert

5 a In pairs, discuss the following questions.
1 Is there a particular ad (film, print, billboard or TV) that you like/dislike at the moment? Describe it, and explain why you like / don't like it.
2 Who is its target audience?
3 How much do you think it cost to produce?
4 How effective do you think it is? Explain your answer.

b ▶7.3 Colleagues from the *Media Design Advertising* agency are having a brainstorming session for *The Daily Sunshine* newspaper advertising campaign. Listen to the meeting and make notes on why the following items are mentioned.
1 Bus
   Suggestion to have people sitting on a bus reading 'The Daily Sunshine' newspaper
2 Truth
3 Free speech
4 Baobab trees
5 Africa
6 Dvořák (a composer)

c In pairs, discuss the meaning of the slogan "*The Daily Sunshine*: Nobody Lies in the Sunshine".

d ▶ 7.3 Listen again and complete the following extracts.

1 So, after a week of deep thought, what _____ _____ _____ ?

2 Any _____ _____ the media campaign?

3 How _____ this picture showing all these people sitting on a bus ...

4 Good idea, but I've got a feeling it's _____ _____ _____ , hasn't it?

5 What have you _____ _____ _____ in the copywriting department?

6 Well, it seems like a good idea, _____ _____ the fact that not everybody knows about ...

7 ... or tell stories. I think we should _____ _____ _____ .

8 Well, if everyone agrees, let's _____ this idea.

9 Well, why _____ _____ limit the time of the TV campaign to 30 seconds only?

10 That's a _____ idea, as long as you can manage to ...

e Add the phrases in Exercise 5d to the following table.

Inviting people to express their ideas	Proposing ideas	Accepting ideas	Rejecting ideas
Any new ideas?	What about ... ? We could ... Let's ...	Sounds good/promising. Sure, why not?	I'm not sure this is what we really need. I don't agree with ...

f Look at the expressions for proposing ideas in the table. Which phrases are followed by a gerund (*-ing*) and which are followed by the infinitive without *to*?

g Complete the following sentences using the correct form of the verb in brackets.

1 We could _____ the image of an old man. (*to use*)

2 How about _____ a close-up shot of somebody reading the paper? (*to do*)

3 Why don't we _____ the ad at sunrise? (*to shoot*)

4 What about _____ a famous actor to endorse our product? (*to get*)

5 Let's _____ viral marketing, too. (*to use*)

6 a In groups, look at these images of baobab trees which have been shortlisted to use in *The Daily Sunshine* campaign and answer the following questions.

1 Which image would you prefer to use for the print ad campaign?
2 Do you agree with the idea that the branches shooting in all directions represent freedom of expression? Explain why / why not.
3 Can you think of a different image to represent the same concept?
4 Can you think of any other slogans that might work with these images?

b In groups, brainstorm ideas for an alternative campaign (for example, a billboard campaign) for *The Daily Sunshine*. Use the language in Exercise 5e.

7 a You are going to read a pre-production meeting (PPM) document for *The Daily Sunshine* TV ad. Before you read, match the words that appear in the text (1–7) to their definitions (a–g).

1	copywriter	a	(in films and TV) the spoken words of a person you cannot see
2	voice-over	b	a series of drawings showing the order of images planned for a film or ad
3	super	c	someone who writes the words for ads
4	shooting storyboard (SS)	d	a series of related things or events, or the order in which they follow each other
5	setting	e	the time and the place in which the action of a book, film, play, etc. happens
6	sequence	f	to make the picture or sound of a film stronger (or weaker)
7	fade in/out	g	slogan appearing on top of an image

b Read the PPM document and match the headings in the box to the corresponding paragraphs (1–8).

Super   Music   Campaign aim   ~~Objective of the PPM~~   Shooting storyboard (SS)
Voice-over   Timetable and logistics   Mood/lighting

Media Design Advertising

Headquarters: Milan, Italy

The Daily Sunshine Ad Campaign
Pre-production Meeting (PPM)
New York, September 1, 2008

IN ATTENDANCE

CLIENT	THE DAILY SUNSHINE	AGENCY	MEDIA DESIGN ADVERTISING, NEW YORK
JOHN MCEWANS	BRAND MANAGER		
FRANCES LOHAN	ASSISTANT BRAND MANAGER	MARIANNE REED	MANAGING DIRECTOR (MD)
		CECILY VALLEY	COPYWRITER
PRODUCTION HOUSE (PH)	**VIDEO RECORDING CAM, PROVIDENCE (RI)**	DAVE TERRY	ART DIRECTOR
JOHN DAVIS	DIRECTOR (D)	EMANUELLE FAITHFUL	TV PRODUCER
ALEXANDER PEACOCK	DIRECTOR OF PHOTOGRAPHY (DOP)	RAFFAELLA LIVINGSTONE	GROUP ACCOUNT MANAGER (GAM)
PETER DOLITTLE	EXECUTIVE PRODUCER (EP)	FRANCIS ROSENTHAL	ACCOUNT SUPERVISOR

AGENDA

1 _Objective of the PPM_
To share and highlight key points regarding *The Daily Sunshine* ad, to be shot at locations and on dates as indicated below.

2 _____
Coordinated publicity to relaunch *The Daily Sunshine*.

3 _____
'Choice of the American people – *The Daily Sunshine* – voted Paper of the Year 2008. A new dawn for journalism. Let *The Daily Sunshine* shed some light on your world.'

4 _____
The Daily Sunshine: Nobody Lies in The Sunshine.

5 _____
It was agreed that the exact nuance for the lighting will be decided on location once the DOP has verified the possible alternatives. It was confirmed that the overall atmosphere should highlight the newspaper through a reveal–suspense sequence.

6 _____
Suspense will be created through slow camera movements and light effects revealing the sun rising among some baobab trees. *The Daily Sunshine* heading will be shown with a fade-in effect, becoming more and more defined. It will then fade out to show the sun up in the sky, before finally revealing the paper's cover in full.

7 _____
Dvořák's *New World Symphony*

8 _____
TV ad to be shot on site in Madagascar on September 25, and at Video Recording Cam studios (Providence) on October 5, by Alexander Peacock. On air from October 30th, the same day as the print campaign.

---

c In pairs, discuss whether you think the commercial will be successful. Explain why / why not.

d In groups, brainstorm a TV ad for the product that you wrote a print ad for in Exercise 4h or another product of your choice. Write your own pre-production meeting document. Use the model in Exercise 7b to help you.

Presenting a finished advert

8 a In pairs, discuss the following questions.

    1 Do you often have to give presentations? If so, what do you present?

    2 Do you enjoy giving presentations? Explain why / why not.

b ▶7.4 Listen to the team at *Media Design Advertising* presenting the TV ad to representatives of *The Daily Sunshine* and answer the following questions.

    1 How many people speak during the meeting?

    2 Do you think the presentation was successful? Explain why / why not.

c ▶7.4 Listen again and complete the following table using the correct headings (a–c).

    a Explaining the details of an ad and saying why it's special

    b Introducing yourself

    c Starting a presentation

1 _____	3 _____
... I'm Marianne Reed, managing director of *Media Design Advertising* ...	... the photography is one of the strong points of this particular piece of work. ... the atmospheric setting and the rising sun represent ... ... the use of classical music ... underlines the fact that this is a serious newspaper. That is what makes this ad campaign so special. We hope the photography will be appreciated because of ... , and also because it ... ... we've come up with a fantastic combination of words and images ...
2 _____ ... if you have any questions, please don't hesitate to interrupt ... Let's begin by watching the advert.	

d Make a list of any more phrases that you think could be added to those in Exercise 8c.

e Imagine you were at the presentation. Write three questions that you would have liked to ask the advertising agency about their ad.

f In groups, think about the TV ad you brainstormed in Exercise 7d. Using those ideas to help you, complete the following sentences.

    1 The ... gets the public's attention.

    2 We hope the ... will be appreciated because ... , and also because it ... .

    3 We have come up with a fantastic ... .

    4 The ... is a strong point of our work.

    5 The ... is what makes this ad campaign so special.

    6 The use of ... underlines the fact that this is a ... .

g In pairs, prepare and role play a presentation for one of the ads you have discussed in this unit. Student A, you represent the advertising agency; Student B, you represent the client. Remember to use the phrases in Exercise 8c to help you. Swap roles and practise again.

h As a class, decide which group had the most effective ad and which pair gave the best presentation.

- Analysing market trends and taking action
- Setting up a marketing communication strategy
- Organising the relaunch of a product
- Evaluating the success of a relaunch

Analysing market trends and taking action

1 **a** **In pairs, discuss the following questions.**

1 Have you ever worked in the marketing or PR (public relations) department of a company? If so, what did you do? If not, what would you like to do?

2 What do you think people who work in PR and marketing do?

b **Look at the following graphs used at a meeting to discuss *Sparkle*, a glossy magazine specialising in jewellery published by *Canada Media*. Which two types of graph are shown: pie chart, line chart or bar chart*?**

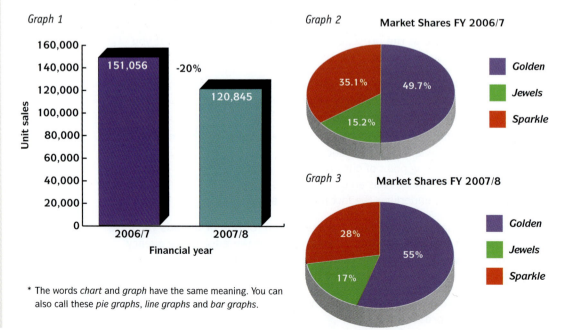

Graph 1

Unit sales / Financial year

151,056 (2006/7) — -20% — 120,845 (2007/8)

Graph 2 **Market Shares FY 2006/7**

49.7% Golden, 35.1% Sparkle, 15.2% Jewels

- Golden
- Jewels
- Sparkle

Graph 3 **Market Shares FY 2007/8**

55% Golden, 28% Sparkle, 17% Jewels

- Golden
- Jewels
- Sparkle

* The words *chart* and *graph* have the same meaning. You can also call these *pie graphs*, *line graphs* and *bar graphs*.

c Look at Graph 1 and then complete the following description of what is shown using the prepositions in the box.

> from   to   ~~with~~   on   by   of

The graph compares unit sales for financial year 2007/8 (1) _with_ sales for financial year 2006/7. Sales fell (2) _____ 30,211 units, (3) _____ 151,056 units during 2006/7 (4) _____ only 120,845 during 2007/8. This represents a decrease (5) _____ 20% (6) _____ the previous year.

d Look at Graphs 2 and 3. What has happened to *Sparkle*'s market share?

2 a ▶8.1 A meeting is taking place at *Canada Media* involving the marketing manager, the market analyst, the director of public relations and the press office manager of *Sparkle*. Listen to the beginning of the meeting and check your answer to Exercise 1d.

b ▶8.1 Listen again and tick (✓) the phrases that you hear.

Talking about trends
Sales are falling.
Profits are improving.
Our losses are increasing.
There's been a dramatic 20% decline in the number of copies sold.
Sales have dropped from 151,056 copies to 120,845.
We lost 7 percentage points of our original market share altogether.
Our competitors' sales have risen by 5 percentage points and 2 percentage points respectively.
Our profits slumped by 27%.

c Decide which of the phrases in the table describe positive change and which describe negative change.

d In pairs, describe the trends shown in Graphs 2 and 3 in Exercise 1b. Use the phrases in Exercise 2b to help you.

e In pairs, discuss the possible reasons for *Sparkle* magazine's loss of market share.

f ▶8.2 The meeting continues. Listen and tick (✓) the things that they discuss.
- ☐ Marketing costs
- ☐ Implementing a new communication strategy
- ☐ Online magazines

g ▶8.3 The meeting comes to a close. Listen and write down at least three suggestions for improving sales of *Sparkle*.

h In pairs, discuss whether you think *Canada Media*'s plan for *Sparkle* will work. Explain why / why not.

3 **a** Complete the following excerpts from the meeting using the words and phrases in the box. Then check your answers using Audioscripts 8.2 and 8.3 on pages 99–100.

> promotion ~~appealing~~ advertising campaign market segment demand needs
> trend report readership boost communication strategy IMC brand awareness

1 It seems that *Sparkle* is simply no longer _appealing_ to readers between 25 and 35. We've virtually lost contact with that _____ .
2 Obviously the problem is with the product itself and to some extent with _____ .
3 We need to raise _____ .
4 We can reverse this negative trend if we look carefully at the four Ps to see where we can increase _____ .
5 We also need to take into account the findings from the competitor analysis and the _____ which were presented to us last week.
6 I also think we need to redesign our overall _____ .
7 We should investigate new communication tools so we can create marketing material that addresses customers' _____ . Integrated marketing communications. That's the solution to the problem – good old _____ .
8 It would be great if we could also have an _____ , wouldn't it?
9 I believe that both of these ingredients will increase our _____ and give a big _____ to our sales.

b Match the beginnings of the definitions (1–8) to the endings (a–h).

1	Communication strategy	a	is a list of the times when events and activities are planned to happen.
2	Activity scheduling	b	is what people think about a company.
		c	is a process used to make sure that all brand contacts received by a customer are relevant to that person and consistent over time.
3	Restyling a magazine involves		
4	The four Ps are	d	is to build a well-rounded marketing mix so as not to overlook anything or concentrate too heavily on any of the Ps in particular.
5	The function of the four Ps		
6	The perception of a company	e	is the extent to which people know and recognise a particular product or brand.
		f	changing photos, font and layout.
7	Brand awareness	g	product, price, place and promotion.
		h	is the identification of strategies for raising brand awareness and improving brand attitudes.
8	IMC		

c In groups, role play a meeting. Student A, you are a marketing manager; Student B, you are a market analyst; Student C, you are a head of PR; and Student D, you are a press office manager. You all work for a magazine which is facing a crisis in its sales due to its old-fashioned format and graphics. Create the graphs of your sales figures. At the meeting, discuss your strategy to improve on these two aspects. Use the language in this section to help you.

Setting up a marketing communication strategy

4 a In pairs, discuss the following questions.

1   What is the difference between the PR department and the press office of a company?
2   How important do you think it is to organise an event when launching a new product?
3   What do you think of famous people endorsing products? Why do companies use celebrity endorsement?

b ▶8.4 One week after their initial meeting, the team at *Canada Media* hold a follow-up meeting. The head of PR and the press office manager are briefing the marketing manager on their activities. Listen to the beginning of the meeting and answer the following questions.

1   What is the main point of discussion?
2   Does everyone at the meeting seem happy?

c ▶8.5 The meeting continues. Listen and find three mistakes in the following activity scheduling document.

Activity Scheduling

Project: *Sparkle* relaunch			
Description	**Next Steps**	**Date**	**Responsible**
Sparkle availability	Relaunched *Sparkle* available on the market	Sep 5 2008	Marketing department
Event	Event to relaunch *Sparkle*	Sep 15	PR dept
Save-the-date	Send save-the-date for event	July	PR dept
Invitation	Send invitations to celebrities, press, advertisers	July	PR dept
Photo shoot	Shoots with celebrities	March	PR dept
Press kit	Including: copy of *Sparkle*, press release, CD containing visuals of advertising campaign	Ongoing	PR dept

---

d ▶8.5 Listen to Audio 8.5 again and complete the following extracts.

Discussing activity scheduling

1   The event _____ _____ _____ our biggest advertisers, the managing directors of top jewellery brands and ...
2   We'll _____ _____ send the invitations by July in order to make sure that they attend.
3   As soon as they're 100% confirmed, we'll _____ _____ _____ for the shoot.
4   But it's also really _____ that we get some positive articles written about the relaunch.
5   ... I assume you're _____ to invite the chief editors of other *Canada Media* magazines to the event ... ?
6   In the _____ , we need to start generating some excitement about the event.
7   We'll have to send the celebrities a save-the-date _____ March.

e ▶8.6 The meeting comes to an end. Listen and answer the following questions.

1   What else is being done to improve *Sparkle*'s sales?
2   How will this be publicised?

f Complete the following definitions using the terms in the box.

> ~~endorsement~~ information sheet save-the-date press kit press release
> product placement

1 A statement made by a famous or important person saying that s/he uses and likes a particular product; alternatively, any public appearance using the product (for example, a celebrity wearing the product): _endorsement_

2 A message sent before a formal invitation is ready which tells people not to make other arrangements for the date of a planned event: _____

3 A written statement which gives information to be broadcast or published: _____

4 A type of advertising where a firm pays to have one of its products appear in a film or TV programme: _____

5 A pre-packaged set of promotional materials distributed to members of the media for promotional use: _____

6 A piece of paper giving details about an item, usually a product: _____

g In groups of five, role play a meeting to set up a communication strategy to relaunch a TV documentary series. The series is called *Headline Weekly* and is a weekly show that reports the headline news in the media world. The show is facing serious problems as its audience share has decreased dramatically. Student A, you are the series director; chair the meeting and make everyone aware of the problems the series faces. Student B, you are the marketing manager; suggest possible reasons for the drop in audience share. Student C, you are the producer; suggest focusing attention on topical media subjects which are of interest to a larger share of the viewers. Students D and E, you are the PR and press office managers; propose a radical change of communication strategy, for example organising a big event.

h When you have finished the discussion, complete the following activity scheduling form.

Activity Scheduling

Project:			
Description	**Next Steps**	**Date**	**Responsible**

Organising the relaunch of a product

5 a In pairs, discuss the following questions.

1 What do you think a good press kit should contain?
2 When might a company choose to use a press kit?
3 Why is the role of the public relations department so important in the organisation of events?

b ▶ 8.7 Shortly before the relaunch of *Sparkle*, the head of PR and the press office manager meet to discuss the progress of the relaunch. Listen to their conversation and tick (✓) the points that they discuss.

☐ Having just a few more deadlines to meet
☐ Proofs (sample pages) for the press kit
☐ Sample designs for the cover
☐ The hard work of everyone on the team
☐ The difficulty in getting testimonials from celebrities
☐ Their next project after the relaunch of *Sparkle*
☐ A slogan for invitation cards

c ▶ 8.7 Listen to the meeting again and tick (✓) the phrases that you hear.

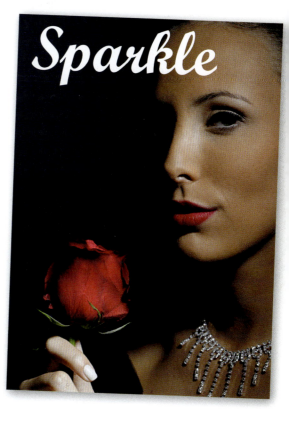

Expressing encouragement
I'd like to thank everybody for their hard work and dedication.
That's good.
I'm sure you're doing an excellent job with the press kit.
It's great.
Excellent!
Keep up the good work.
Great job!
Well done to you and all of your team.
I'm really impressed with the way you've organised the event.
That's brilliant work.
Good stuff. You've done really well so far.

d In pairs, discuss the following questions.

1 What did they say about the photo chosen for the September issue of *Sparkle*? Do you agree with them?
2 In pairs, discuss whether you would use this cover to relaunch *Sparkle* or not. Discuss the font used in the title and the overall visual impact that this combination may have on readers.

e In pairs, role play a follow-up meeting based on your meeting in Exercise 4g. Student A, you are the head of PR; get an update from the press office manager and give encouragement as appropriate. Student B, you are the press office manager; update the head of PR on the progress you've made on your new communication strategy.

6 **a** **In pairs, discuss the following questions.**

1   What is a press release? Who and what is it for?
2   How is a press release delivered?

b **Complete the following press release using the section headings in the box.**

> Expert advice   Accessing the product   Historical background
> Target market   Innovative approach

CanadaMedia

Contact: Maggie Donaldson   **FOR IMMEDIATE RELEASE**
Tel: 1.877.826.1917
Email: m_donaldson@CanMedia.ca

CANADA MEDIA GROUP TO RELAUNCH LUXURY MAGAZINE
Putting the spark back into *Sparkle*

1   _____

Sparkle first appeared in the mid-1970s. It was the only publication covering jewellery in Canada at the time and one of the very few of its kind in the world. Its claim to fame is its history of getting the inside story on some of the most famous and influential designers in the world.

2   _____

Its new, stylish, colourful layout is a completely innovative approach. It has a new font, advanced graphics, and eye-catching photography. These features contribute further to enhance the timeless beauty of jewellery which combines contemporary creativity with traditional motifs.

3   _____

Sparkle is now aimed not only at the traditional buyers – mature, sophisticated women – but also at younger women (25–35).

4   _____

What's more, our exciting new fashion guru, Samantha Hollinghurst, will be providing advice and ideas on how to combine the latest jewellery designs with the rest of your wardrobe – whether it's for a black-tie cocktail party or simply to wear to the office.

5   _____

The new *Sparkle* will be available from all the usual sales outlets, and from next October readers will also be able to browse our new online edition.

c **Read the press release again. Look at the highlighted adjectives and answer the following questions.**

1   How would you describe the adjectives used?
   ● effective   ● unnecessary   ● negative   ● powerful
2   How would you describe the sentence structure?
   ● colourful   ● short   ● formal   ● focused
3   Why do you think the writer used these kinds of adjectives and this type of sentence structure?

d **Write a press release based on the role play in Exercise 5e, using the headings in Exercise 6b. Before you start, underline all the useful phrases in the press release in Exercise 6b which you could use in your own press release.**

Evaluating the success of a relaunch

7 a In pairs, discuss the following questions.

    1   Have you ever been involved in reporting the results of a project you've worked on? If so, how did you find the experience?

    2   Why is the sale of advertising space so important for magazines and newspapers?

b After the relaunch of *Sparkle*, there is a meeting to analyse the communication strategy used and the effect it is having on sales. Tick (✓) the items you think will be discussed.

- ☐ Effect on revenue from the sale of advertising space
- ☐ Impact of celebrities' presence at the event
- ☐ Response of the press
- ☐ Feedback from advertisers
- ☐ Public's response to product placement

c ▶ 8.8 Listen to the meeting and see if your predictions were correct.

d ▶ 8.8 Listen again and decide if the following statements are True (T) or False (F).

    1   The meeting has been called to analyse the impact of the relaunch plan on sales.

    2   Only twenty people attended the event organised to launch *Sparkle*.

    3   The newspaper coverage received by the launch of *Sparkle* is not very good.

    4   *Sparkle* has regained 1.2 percentage points of the market share lost in the previous year.

    5   The marketing manager seems happy with how the relaunch has gone.

e Complete the following extracts from the meeting by writing the correct tense of the verbs in the box.

> regain   receive (x2)   manage   be (x4)   see

Analysing feedback

1   Our efforts __have been__ very successful in general.

2   ... the restyled version of *Sparkle* _____ a hit.

3   The feedback we _____ from advertisers so far is very encouraging ...

4   ... the advertising revenue from selling space in the magazine _____ very good so far.

5   ... we _____ to reverse the trend.

6   ... according to the latest report I _____ this morning from the Marketing Analysis department, ...

7   ... *Sparkle*'s print run _____ gradually increasing.

8   ... we _____ a 4% gain in copies sold.

9   This also means we _____ 1.12 percentage points of the market share we lost ...

---

f In pairs, discuss why sentence 6 above uses the past simple instead of present perfect.

g **Read an article about the relaunch of *Sparkle* from a trade magazine and answer the following questions.**

1 Is the writer positive or negative about the new version of *Sparkle*?
2 Can you find any factual errors in the article?

A real gem!

by Cindy Nicholson

In an ever-changing and varied media world, the rich confirm they have always been a niche market.

Jewel lovers rejoice! *Canada Media*, publisher of three luxury magazines, are relaunching their famous high-end glossy magazine, *Sparkle*. Magazines that cater to the affluent are not new, but, since its launch in 1986, *Sparkle* has always been one of the most prestigious and successful of them. Now the Head of Publishing at *Canada Media*, Diana Williams, says it is about time to regain the interest of younger readers in *Sparkle*. She maintains that this can be done by "strengthening the awareness of *Sparkle* and by reinforcing the perception of its image."

I'm pleased to say that the new-look issue has a highly innovative format and wonderful graphics, accompanied by some outstanding photography. In this way,

Canada Media hopes to attract not only a larger readership, but also some of the top luxury advertisers.

Product placement is another asset that the team at *Sparkle* have managed to use effectively, both on TV and in films. Besides the brilliant idea to have Claudia Schneider and Nicole Lopez at the launch event, what's been even more important is getting both of them to endorse *Sparkle* in a recent advert.

Distribution will follow the model of the company's other magazines: top newspaper stands in the most affluent quarters in the big cities, and subscriptions in North America. However, the great novelty is a new browsable online version of *Sparkle*, which it is hoped will be particularly popular among young women. The online version should be available in February.

h **In pairs, discuss the following questions.**

1 Why do you think positive press coverage is so important when products are being launched or relaunched?
2 Do you think that when it comes to launching new products, the saying that "all publicity is good publicity" is still true? Explain why / why not.

i **In groups, role play a meeting to discuss feedback about the communication strategy you adopted in Exercise 4g. Student A, you are the marketing manager; chair the meeting and illustrate any positive trends in sales since the implementation of the communication strategy. Student B, you are head of PR; comment on figures about any events you organised (for example, number of attendees, content of press kit, press coverage and response). Student C, you are the press office manager; you are enthusiastic about the significant revenue increase coming from increased advertising sales.**

AUDIOSCRIPT

1.1

Interviewer: Hello. I'm Simon Young, *Express Times*, pleased to meet you.

Katie: Pleased to meet you. Please, take a seat.

Interviewer: Thank you for agreeing to talk to me. As I said in my email, we want to do a profile on women in the media for our weekly media supplement.

Katie: I'm very flattered to be asked. Fire away.

Interviewer: OK. I've done my background research but could you go over your career to date?

Katie: Sure. After university I did a Postgraduate Diploma course in Newspaper Journalism and then worked as a trainee for a local weekly newspaper based in Southsea—

Interviewer: Sorry to interrupt, but how long did the postgraduate course last and where did you do it?

Katie: Right. Um … it lasted a year and I did it in Cardiff. A great course but really hard work.

Interviewer: Good preparation for journalism! And then?

Katie: Right, er, like I said … after the course, I worked as a trainee for *The Southsea Times*, a local weekly newspaper, for 12 months. I transferred to another weekly paper, *Hatherfield Herald*, for another 12 months, where I worked as a reporter and then sub-editor. Then I joined *The Southern Mail*, first as a district news reporter, then the education correspondent, one of the assistant news editors, and finally the deputy news editor. I left *The Southern Mail*—

Interviewer: Sorry to butt in again. You had four different positions at *The Southern Mail*?

Katie: Yes, that's right.

Interviewer: And did you enjoy the positions?

Katie: Like any job they had their advantages and disadvantages.

Interviewer: What exactly were they?

Katie: Good experience. Long hours.

Interviewer: Then what did you do?

Katie: Then I left *The Southern Mail* to work for UK Radio Wales, where I produced a series of news programmes including The Afternoon Show.

Interviewer: Did you—

Katie: Did I enjoy that experience? Let's just say by the end I was glad to leave.

Interviewer: Could you be more specific?

Katie: No. I'd rather not.

Interviewer: OK. So then?

Katie: Where was I? … Oh yes … after UK Radio Wales I got my present job as head of the press office for Bristol Council – a job which I really enjoy because of the variety and hours.

Interviewer: And your future plans? Will you continue as head of the press office or are you looking for a new position?

Katie: No. I intend to stay here for quite a while, as I'm still enjoying the variety the job offers.

Interviewer: The variety, right. … So you've been involved with the media, and more specifically newspapers, for nearly two decades …

Katie: Hmm.

1.2

Interviewer: Have newspapers changed during your career?

Katie: Yes, especially the content.

Interviewer: Why do you say that?

Katie: Well, newspapers have far less in-depth content now than 20 years ago, with more emphasis on the lighter, celebrity-based stories.

Interviewer: And how would you describe the present newspaper market in the UK?

Katie: It's a tough market. The majority of newspapers are not seeing rises in their circulation any more and all have had to diversify and consider how best they might present their news to their readers. Large newspaper companies are training their reporters to use camcorders so they can provide footage for websites. Online news is the way a lot of the public want to receive information. Then the newsroom is a difficult place to work at the moment. Lots of journalists are losing their jobs because, as I'm sure you know, newspapers don't make money out of editorial but out of advertising. This means journalists are seen as quite disposable.

Interviewer: So, is the era of print newspapers coming to an end?

Katie: The romantic in me says print newspapers will always exist, as they are a unique chronicle of daily life across the globe, and a fantastic reference for future generations. The pragmatist in me says it's quite an outdated mode of receiving information and one which may not survive the digital age.

Interviewer: Who is your media inspiration?

Katie: This is a tough question. I think Henry Linton, the veteran foreign correspondent for UK Radio, is excellent. The best.

Interviewer: Finally, do you have any advice for people starting out in the world of journalism?

Katie: Well, the most important piece of advice I can give them is …

2.1

1 We've still got Madonna's *Ray of Light* to play for you, and a track from The Beatles, but first, the Foo Fighters, *Learn to Fly*.

2 Let's talk to Jonathan White, our football correspondent.

3 **Male voice:** It's 6 o'clock on Monday the 24th of September. This is *The Morning Show*, with John Gray in London and Samantha Martin in Bournemouth.

   Female voice: Hello. I'm here at the Labour Party Conference where the Prime Minister will announce new laws to combat gun crime. We'll be speaking to the Prime Minister at ten past eight.

   Male voice: And the other news. Vets are checking more animals to see if there are any more cases of mad cow disease. Also, anti-government student protests are planned for the capital today and, finally, should robots look after the elderly?

4 It's 8 o'clock, and you're having breakfast with me, Amanda Green. Coming up, more information about the London Jazz Festival, but now over to the newsroom.

5 And now it's time for *Everyday Women*, our daily look at women's issues, with Carla Morris.

6 Here's the second movement of Beethoven's *Emperor Concerto*, performed by the Berlin Philharmonic Orchestra and conducted by Heinrich Erhard.

7 **Female voice:** I'm Gemma Wilson and welcome to *In Focus*, our weekly cultural documentary. This week, Rahim Anwar presents a programme about the poet Auden to mark the centenary of his birth. We're going to explore his life, work and popularity.

   Male voice: Hello. Auden became the spokesmen of a generation …

8 I'm Mo Ace and this is a free podcast. This week's documentary is all about the music genius that is Dr Dre.

2.2

1 You're listening to Radio Australia. I'm Gil Brennen and welcome to *Good Morning Australia*.

2 Here's Bach's Concerto for keyboard in D major, performed by Colm Carey.

3 It's Tuesday the 19th January. This is *Report*, with Bill Noles and Justine Welsh. Still to come in the next half hour, we'll be interviewing Janie Kirk.

4 That was Coldplay with *Viva la vida*. Before that, you heard *Rockstar* by Nickelback.

5 This week, John Walsh presents a programme about finding work on the Internet.

2.3

Dawn Henderson: Good morning, all. We've got a lot to do today so let's get straight down to business. Can we look at the first half-hour section of the programme? Peter, I want you to work on the item about rising house prices. You'll need to find some good examples to illustrate this. Also, I'd like an interview with an estate agent and a package with a first-time house buyer explaining how difficult it is to buy their first house. For the estate agent, contact Pierce Wright at *Homeseller's*; he's on our database. As for first-time house buyers, I'm sure you'll have no trouble finding one.

Peter: Too right, I'll just ask around the office! Should I also look into the possible increase in mortgages?

Dawn: Only if it adds to the story. Madeline, can you deal with the piece about school closures? I'd like you to invite a leading educationalist onto the programme. There's a woman at Western University that we've used before – Professor Lyle, I think. Also, I want you to organise a phone link-up with parents involved in a protest group to keep their school open.

Madeline: Do you mean parents plural, or will one parent be enough?

Dawn: You decide, but remember to keep it snappy. I'm going to get in a stringer for the story on the opening of the latest Picasso Museum in France. Elsa, you get the story about the recent forest fires and a possible connection with global warming. Speak to *Friends of the Earth*, a top meteorologist, and take it from there.

▮ 2.4

Sarah Bernard: Âllo?

Dawn: Hi, Sarah. It's Dawn Henderson from *Good Morning Australia*. How are you?

Sarah: Not too bad. And you?

Dawn: Mad busy as always. I'm calling you as we need a story for tomorrow's programme about the new Picasso museum in France.

Sarah: OK. So what can I do for you?

Dawn: I've read that there's some controversy because it's opening in a building which was previously used as a night shelter where homeless people could sleep.

Sarah: Yes, that's right.

Dawn: OK, so I want you to write me a short script outlining the issues and find me two people who we can link up with live, one who represents the museum and one who represents the homeless people. You'll also need to write interview questions and brief them on what we'll ask. They'll be needed on air between 6 and 7 am Australian time. Can you do it, and are you interested? The payment will be the standard fee.

Sarah: Sure. When do you need the story for?

Dawn: We'll need the script and contact numbers by 4 pm our time at the latest.

Sarah: OK. I'll get onto it right away. I'll email you the script and contact numbers ASAP.

Dawn: Great. Thanks. Have a good day.

Sarah: Bye.

▮ 2.5

Dawn: So let's get the ball rolling. Who wants to comment first on this morning's show? Jim, perhaps?

Jim: Well, obviously the studio going down for several seconds, and the show being off air was not a great moment. We're still trying to figure out what happened.

Dawn: Do you have any idea what the cause was and how we can avoid it happening again in the future?

Jim: As I said, it's still a mystery, but my guess is that it was a problem with the electricity current. As soon as we know the cause, I'll let you know.

Dawn: OK. Elsa, what happened to the meteorology expert?

Elsa: I've just spoken to him. He says he was stuck in traffic.

Dawn: For the entire programme?

Elsa: He said that he tried to phone on several occasions, but he couldn't get through. I've no record of him calling me. Personally, I think he forgot to set his alarm clock. He sounded very sleepy when he answered his home phone.

Dawn: Well, we'll know not to use him again. On a positive note, I think you'll agree getting an eyewitness account of the rail crash was a real scoop. I was also very happy with the piece about house prices, and I think the piece on the Picasso museum was well done.

▮ 3.1

In this month's issue, beat the heat: great summer fashion. Plus, shape up and show off: get bikini ready – fast!

▮ 3.2

1 Make your house clean and green!
2 Get fit and fabulous! The best exercises for brides-to-be!
3 Spanish special: tasty tapas recipes and magical Madrid gourmet guide
4 Fun in the sun: ten top holiday destinations
5 Matt Damon's killer instinct: why we prefer Bourne to Bond
6 Beijing rising
7 What to wear from 19 to 91

▮ 3.3

Jane Lawson (editor-in-chief): OK, as nearly everybody's here – Joanne texted me to say she's going to be late – let's get down to work. It's April so we've got to start thinking about July's issue. As usual, I asked you to come up with various proposals. So, who's going to start?

Richard O'Donnell (deputy editor): I'd like to remind everyone that in July there are the World Championships in Rio so any stories and features linking to that would be good.

Charlotte Smith-Hughes (fashion editor): Well, actually, I'd like to propose a piece on Rio fashion designers, as there are lots of young, exciting designers there who I think are going to be really big names in the future. It might be expensive, but it would tie in nicely with the World Championships. Also, a lot of celebrities have been seen wearing the latest designs by a couple of the designers I have in mind.

Jane: I don't know. What about the logistics?

Charlotte: That's not a problem. I'll contact the photographer and stylist we used for the shoot we did in Brazil last year. Remember what incredible photos we came out with?

Jane: Mm. I think it's a great idea if you can keep within budget. Can you check out how much it'll cost and get back to me?

Charlotte: Sure thing. I'll do it immediately.

Jane: OK, what do you have for the food section, Scott?

Scott Fisher (features editor): I'd like to commission a couple of short pieces. One on vegetarian food—

Lisa Swan (art director): What, 500 words about beans!

Jane: OK, folks, let's get back to the point.

*   *   *

Jane: Right, I think we've got some good ideas. Let's go over what we've decided so far.

Sally (secretary): Sorry to interrupt, but you're needed urgently.

Jane: Urgently?

Sally: Yes.

Jane: I guess I'd better go then. Excuse me, all. I'll hand you over to Richard. Richard?

Richard: No problem … Grace is going to do a short round-up of beach destinations in Rio, and Denise is going to do a true story feature about a couple who fell in love on holiday in Rio, lost touch for thirty years, and then found each other again by chance. And we've got vegetarian food and Rio fashion designers. Have I covered everything? Then that's about it. I just want to finish by going over deadlines. The 21st of April is the deadline for the commissioning of any articles. Copy deadline is the 19th of May. Artwork needs to go to the printer by the 30th of May. Publication for the July issue is the 14th of June. Has everyone got that? … That's all. Don't forget we're meeting here on Thursday at 10 am for the final decisions on what's in and what's out.

▮ 3.4

1
A: Can you believe it? I'm interviewing Matt Damon tomorrow. I'm so nervous! He's always been one of my favourite actors.

B: Lucky you! Can I come too?

2
C: I'm never going to have the piece finished for the 19th.

D: Don't worry about the deadline. It's been extended. It's the 23rd, not the 19th.

C: That's good news!

3
E: Do you have time to go for lunch?

F: Not really. But why not. I'll proofread the copy when I get back. OK, let's go. What do you fancy?

E: Let's go to the sandwich bar on the corner.

4
G: What can I do for you?

H: A lot, actually. I'd really like to know when I'm going to be paid!

G: Well, um … er ….

▮ 3.5

Charlotte: Well, actually, I'd like to propose a piece on Rio fashion designers, as there are lots of young, exciting designers there who I think are going to be really big names in the future. It might be expensive, but it would tie in nicely with the World Championships. Also, a lot of celebrities have been seen wearing the latest designs by a couple of the designers I have in mind.

Jane: I don't know. What about the logistics?

Charlotte: That's not a problem. I'll contact the photographer and stylist we used for the shoot we did in Brazil last year. Remember what incredible photos we came out with?

▮ 3.6

a Let's get back to the point.
b Let's go over what we've decided.
c I'll hand you over to Richard.
d Have I covered everything?

▮ 3.7

1
You're through to the *Photo Shoot Agency*. We're sorry that nobody is able to take your call at the moment. Please leave a message and your details, and we'll get back to you as soon as possible.

Hello. This is Charlotte Smith-Hughes, the fashion editor of *Glorious* magazine. I'm calling to check that you've received the contract and the brief for the shoot on the 5th of June. Could you please ring me back on 0207 478274 to confirm that you've received them. Thank you.

2
Hi, this is Steve. I can't speak right now. Leave me a message.

Hi, Steve. It's Charlotte. I've sent you the contract and the brief for our upcoming shoot. Give me a ring to confirm that you've received both of them. My work number is 0207 478274. Speak to you soon.

4.1

Victoria: Good morning. Let's get started. You'll find my ideas about last night in the email I sent. Just to say I thought the package on the Prime Minister was excellent, and the live footage from Georgia with the Scotland football squad was great. So well done on that. Donna's producing today. What have you got for us, Donna?

Donna: Lots of stuff on the wires. Reuters is reporting that a terrorist has made a video threatening foreign embassies. The twist is that this guy's an American. Also, it's First Minister's Questions in the Scottish Parliament today. Our political editor's saying that the Opposition will be complaining about the lack of police on the streets again. A flood has killed 330 people in South-east Asia, so there's serious concern about disease there. We should be getting a package from our Asia correspondent who's in Bangladesh at the moment. There's a great story in Birmingham about human trafficking. The police raided a suspected building there as part of a big operation to crack down on people involved in the trade of humans. They've got DV footage that they shot themselves available for us, and it's horrific stuff. The conditions these people have been kept in are absolutely terrible.

Neil: It would be great if we could get the story as an exclusive, wouldn't it?

Donna: Yes, definitely, Neil. I'll look into that. Anyway, those are the main news events. What do you think?

Victoria: The American terrorist video has got to be the top story. Could we get a package and a live from the Washington bureau?

Donna: Yeah, that shouldn't be a problem. I've already asked for a correspondent.

Neil: Er, Andrew, can we get a Scottish angle on the trafficking story?

Andrew: Sure. I could get an interview with a woman I know who was trafficked from Eastern Europe to London but who managed to get away and is now living in Glasgow. I'll talk to the Serious Crimes Agency as well to find out how big a problem trafficking is in Scotland. I could pack it up using the police footage from Birmingham. I think it'd be great if we could produce a whole programme on this issue here and abroad by using our own camera crews.

Victoria: I'll see what we can do about that. It sounds good to me. It would be an excellent start for the next winter series of our current affairs programme, *Bird's Eye View*. In the meantime, we'll put our top reporters, Andrew and Neil, on to getting people's views on the trafficking issue. So, going back to our news programme, Donna, what's the running order?

Donna: Well, for the moment I'll go with terrorism, trafficking, First Minister's Questions in the Scottish Parliament, floods in Bangladesh. OK? Let's meet back here at 2.30.

4.2

Donna: Hello, everybody. Great news! Victoria has just told me that our pitch for the trafficking documentary has been approved. Last time we spoke about this, we were thinking about an hour-long programme with three elements, weren't we? I think that's still the best way to go. We could talk to trafficked people now living in various EU countries about their experiences. We should also interview the police and find some experts who can talk about how big the problem is across Europe. I think then we'll have to travel to some European countries where these people are trafficked from to find out why it's happening.

Neil: Yes, I think that's the way to go. I've been talking to Andrew Preston, the social affairs correspondent in the newsroom, who can help us with our primary research. He's confirmed he can help us get in touch with several women who've escaped trafficking. I've passed the details on to Sylvana.

Sylvana: Yeah, I spoke to two women and did pre-interviews with them on the phone. Their stories are really awful, but they don't come across as victims. They're really strong women. They'll be great interviewees. But, we must remember to be sensitive during the interview. We don't want them to feel uncomfortable with any of the questions.

Donna: Good. The primary research all looks very promising. But how have you been getting on with your secondary research? We'd better not forget that.

Sylvana: Don't worry, I've got lots of footage and interviews that I found in our archives and several stories from the print media. I found a really interesting report by *Europol* that was given to the European Parliament as well.

Donna: OK, that sounds good. You'll need to write all that up in a brief for us, but you don't have to go into too much detail, OK?

Sylvana: Yeah, no problem.

James: I was thinking about ways of making the story more interesting visually, instead of just having a lot of talking heads.

Donna: Have you got any ideas yet?

James: I don't know exactly, but I was thinking of shooting some moody footage of border posts and cars crossing borders. Maybe filming from underneath a blanket so you get the viewpoint of someone being smuggled through. That kind of thing.

Donna: OK, sounds good. Let's meet again tomorrow to see where we are.

4.3

1

Donna: Penny, have you checked if all our interviewees have signed these forms? We don't want anyone to think they can claim payment later.

Penny: Don't worry, everybody's signed.

2

Donna: And are the crew aware how much money they can spend each day while we're away?

Penny: Yes, I've already briefed them on that.

Donna: Good! I don't want anyone to go hungry, but last time we filmed on location some of the crew spent far too much in madly expensive restaurants! I mean, we do have a limit!

Penny: It's OK, everyone knows exactly how much they can spend per day.

3

Donna: Oh, just one more thing before we go to the airport. We'll never get the PSC or digital MP3 recorder through customs if we can't show the official documents we need.

Penny: Relax, Donna. All the documents are in order.

4

Penny: By the way, the camera operator says he's really pleased with the camera because it takes digibeta tapes. That's exactly what we need for this type of documentary.

Donna: We'd better make sure we've got plenty of tape with us.

Penny: Of course. I've arranged for that.

4.4

Donna: OK, James, just remind me what we've got so far.

James: I've got the tracking shots of the countryside that we took from the car. I've also got the GVs of the border crossing that you asked for – nice slow pans across the countryside, nice tilts from the border post up to the blue sky, pull focus shots from the car wing mirror to the guard post, the POV stuff from under the blanket in the back seat, and the sequences of driving up to the border point and having the passport looked over closely.

Donna: Were the border guards OK about being filmed, Stefan?

Stefan: Well, actually they were a bit nervous about being involved in the filming at first, but I spoke to their officer and showed them our passes from the Interior Ministry. They're happy to help out now. No big problem.

Donna: That's great. How would we manage without you? OK, I think we should get down to the PTC now. Neil, are you ready?

Neil: Yes, I've written down what I'm going to say. Where do you want me?

Donna: I think it'd be good to have you doing a walkie-talkie from next to the guard post, down parallel to the crossing barrier towards the camera sited just about here. What do you think, James? If you have a better idea, please tell us.

James: No, your suggestion is great, I think that'll work really well. We'll need to get the guards to hold the traffic for a bit, though. And it might be a bit windy for the personal mic. We might need to put the big windshield on it.

Donna: We'll give it a go and see what the sound's like. Stefan, could you tell the guards what we want to do, please?

Stefan: No problem.

4.5

Donna: Hi, Diana.

Diana: Hi, Donna. You made it back then?

Donna: Eventually! What a nightmare! So, how's it going?

Diana: We're still editing the human trafficking documentary. Yesterday I concentrated on the section where you were on location. I started off with some GVs and tracking shots, then moved on to the interviews you did.

Donna: Are there any interesting ones?

Diana: There's one interview with a woman who was trafficked that's really powerful. I followed your suggestion in your email and intercut it with some sequences you shot at the border. The idea is that it's almost like a reconstruction of someone being trafficked. I thought it would be good to use a lot of slow mixes so that we get a dreamy feel. What do you think?

Donna: Yeah, I'll have a look. You know, sometimes with sequences like that it's better to use cuts. Ah, Neil! You made it! Are you feeling better now? I wasn't expecting to see you today.

Neil: Yes, I'm much better, thanks.

Donna: So, have you decided what sections of interview you're using?

Neil: Yes, I think so. Diana, did you say that you'd done some work with the clipspotter yesterday?

Diana: Yes, and I've got all the time codes here. Any music?

Donna: Yeah, I've got this track here and some low drones from this royalty-free compilation CD I told you about. Have a listen to it later.

Diana: It's great working with you, Donna. You're so organised! I bet you've even got a list of the shots you took on location!

Donna: Yep. Here's one I prepared earlier!

Neil: Listen, Donna, can I record my voice now? The newsroom want me to cover a story in Liverpool, so I'll need to leave in about two hours to be there on time. We've agreed the script.

Diana: We recorded Sylvana earlier today as we thought you might be too ill.

Donna: It doesn't matter. We'll record Neil now he's here. The booth's all set up for you, Neil. Just head in and we'll fix an appropriate voice level.

▇▇ 5.1

Film Executive 1: Good afternoon. Come in and take a seat.

Jamie Louis: Hello.

Film Executive 1: I trust you had no problem getting here?

Jamie: No, no problem.

Film Executive 2: So, is this your first screenplay?

Jamie: Actually, no. This is my second. My first screenplay made it into the top ten of the Nicholl Fellowships in Screenwriting competition and is currently under option with a Hollywood studio.

Film Executive 1: Impressive stuff. So what have you got for us?

Jamie: Well, I'd like to tell you about my latest piece.

Film Executive 1: Fire away.

Jamie: OK. So, my film's called *on stAGE*. It's a touching musical comedy set in the North of England. This is a story about a group of men who, on turning 40, decide to re-form their teenage band but find that teenage values and ideas aren't always the same across generations. On guitar there's Peter, the eternal woman's man; on bass guitar there's Johnny, the eternal rebel; on drums, there's the family man, Brian; and on vocals there's recently divorced Gus, who's involved in constant generational disagreements with his 17-year-old son, Jake. As these four men try to relive their youth, the different lifestyles and personalities make for lots of poignant comedy situations.

Film Executive 1: Uh-huh.

Jamie: But then disaster strikes. Gus is killed in a road accident. Jake, Gus's son, takes his father's place, makes peace with the memory of his father and his father's generation, and the film ends with him leading the group to success in a local talent contest. *on stAGE*, get it? *on stAGE* – *age* in capital letters. The band on stage and the age – the generational difference. This film is aimed at an audience in the 20–50 age group. There are a number of great rock scenes which are accompanied by a wonderful soundtrack of classic songs from the last three decades. *on stAGE* is a feelgood film which combines tears and laughter. I'm confident it will generate lots of critical and box office success. Think *Spinal Tap* meets *The Breakfast Club*. Think Nick Hornby does Bridget Jones.

Film Executive 2: That all sounds very interesting, but could you explain how the audience is expected to believe that the son will go and play in his father's band?

Jamie: Well, the screenplay actually gives two motives. One, the son needs a distraction, and the band provides this. Secondly, the relationship between Gus and Jake, as you can read in the screenplay is, despite the disagreements and arguments, very strong.

Film Executive 2: Hm. OK. Do you have any questions for Jamie?

Film Executive 1: No, I think I've got a clear idea of where this screenplay is going. If you leave a copy with us, we'll get back to you within a couple of weeks.

Jamie: Right, thanks, er, could I ask …

▇▇ 5.2

Indira: OK, folks, so now we need to focus on the final preparations. I've already undertaken a reconnoitre on location, and there are practically no problems with access for teams and equipment, and, most importantly, electricity is available almost everywhere. My next recces will be aimed at checking on health and safety in case anything happens while we're on location, and the setting up of facilities like bathrooms and a PR and press office. As for the creative side of the production, I'll let our director, Kirpal, tell you about that.

Kirpal: Well, my main concern at this stage is that whatever locations we select, we need to bear in mind how they will look on film; and we also need to avoid any problems that may slow down shooting. Rajeshwar, as director of photography, is there anything you can tell us about this?

Rajeshwar: I've done a couple of recces at key locations, and I'm a little concerned about the lighting for the scenes that will be shot in the Caves of Maharashtra, and those in certain open-air sites such as the jungle. However, after careful consideration, my camera crew think the problem can be solved with extra lighting rigs in the caves and filters that reduce the amount of light let into the camera. I'm taking it for granted that electricity will be provided by two generators.

Kirpal: OK. I'll try to get you the most advanced generators we can. How about you, Latha, do you have any problems with these locations?

Latha: No, none at all. Actually, sound conditions are excellent. Knowing there will be a screaming scene, when we reconnoitred all the sites one of the sound crew screamed to check the natural sound effects. The echoes sounded for several seconds. Actually, the result was so impressive that we all agreed we wouldn't be able to reproduce anything better in the studio. In the jungle, too, everything seems to be so perfectly set: the birds singing, the sound of animals, the wind blowing among the tree branches every now and then.

Kirpal: Great. Er, Indira, just one more thing. Have you already asked the local authorities for permission to film at the Taj Mahal and the Maharashtra Caves? I'd like to start shooting these two scenes as soon as possible.

Indira: Actually, because we need to shoot in so many different locations, I've decided to contact our usual location agency, *Filmfactory*. They have lots of experience in location management and production. They'll contact local authorities and private location owners and can provide us with advice and support if we need …

▇▇ 6.1

1 w-w-w dot the Scottish bookshop dot com
2 Gavin underscore Bennett at the Scottish bookshop dot com

▇▇ 6.2

Paolo: So, you were given my name by Julie? She tells me that you're keen to get your physical shop onto the web.

Ian: Yeah, that's right. I don't know if she also told you that neither of us are particularly web-savvy, so you'll have to keep your explanations simple.

Paolo: She did mention it, but that's what I'm here for! We could start by thinking about what it is you want to achieve with your website. I assume you want a site that will enable you to sell books online?

Fiona: That's right. Nowadays a web presence is absolutely necessary, especially in the retail industry. We need to showcase our stock, and at the same time, our shop in Glasgow.

Paolo: Right. Do you have any ideas of what domain name you'd like?

Fiona: Domain *what*, sorry? What's that?

Paolo: It's the address of your website. It's important to keep it simple. We should try to get www.thescottishbookshop.com. I've checked with a company which offers web hosting services that I think you should use, and the name is available.

Ian: It's my turn to be confused. What exactly are web hosting services?

Paolo: A web hosting service is a type of service which allows individuals and organisations to set up their own websites. They're companies that provide space on a server – a server is a kind of computer system which provides specific programs or applications.

Ian: OK. So my new virtual shop would be stored on a server by the web hosting service, and I don't have to worry about running my own servers or anything like that.

Paolo: That's right. You'll pay a monthly fee, and they'll take care of all the technical infrastructure, which allows you to focus on selling books. So, let's start thinking about what you would like to include in your new web shop …

Paolo: … so we've decided that on the home page you want a shopping basket, a customer log in, a drop-down menu of book categories and bookshop information, images of the latest releases, a search function, and possibly a short text about the shop. This brings up a few considerations. Firstly, how many images do you want to include? Before broadband the more images you included, the slower the download time was, but that's no longer a problem. And secondly, who's going to be responsible for maintaining the site? If you include all these features, you'll need someone to do web maintenance – you know, keep the catalogue up-to-date and reply to enquiries.

Ian: Yeah, we'd realised that this was going to be complicated, but fortunately our son Gareth, who is on holiday this week, is much more IT literate than us. I'm sure that once he understands the system, he'll be able to take care of these responsibilities. In fact, it's a real shame that he can't be here for this initial meeting, but he'll be present at future meetings.

Fiona: Julie said you might be able to help us out with the initial maintenance or suggest someone who can.

Paolo: Sure, that won't be a problem. I'll email you a quote in the next couple of days, and if you're happy with my price we can take it from there.

Fiona: Great. It's been really interesting talking to you.

Ian: Yeah, I look forward to doing business with you and getting our website up and running. Thanks for coming here today. Have a safe journey.

Paolo: Thanks. Bye.

6.3

Ben: Hello, everyone, and welcome to the latest *Notes from Spain* podcast. Today we're going to be talking about setting up an online business in Spain.

Marina: Hello.

Ben: Now, the first thing you're going to need to know is that most of the accountants you come across here aren't used to working with online businesses. Why is that, Marina?

Marina: In Spain, there is not much … there are not much online businesses apart from the big companies. And also, buying on the Internet depends on age. Older people – people like my parents, for example – never buy on the Internet.

Ben: Yeah, whereas my dad, who is 65, is buying a lot on the Internet. So, problem number one is that you will probably have to find an accountant who is willing to take on the responsibility of the online side of things.

Marina: … to learn, yeah …

Ben: Really that involves two sides. Number one: processing payments. For example, payments for our Spanish site come in by *Paypal*, and we had to work closely with the accountant to work out how we would take our *Paypal* receipts and process them onto paper in a way that he could understand. Now, the other problem is that the accountant is going to have to work with you and a lawyer to draw up a privacy policy. Marina, what is this privacy policy and why is it so important?

Marina: Well, you need to protect the data you receive from your clients.

Ben: OK.

Marina: And to do so you have to fill in a file for the data protection agency.

Ben: Yeah.

Marina: And in that file you need to more or less explain what information you collect from your clients and what you use this information for.

Ben: So, for example, on our website, visitors can leave comments on articles we write. And the simple fact that people write their name, their email address and their comment on our website, which then gets stored on our servers, means we have to declare this fact in our privacy policy to the data protection agency. I was pretty amazed by the fact that you had to declare people are leaving comments on your website! So this privacy policy is submitted not only to the data protection agency, but you also need it on your website.

Marina: That's right. Then there are things like terms and conditions agreements for the store part of our website.

Ben: Which we put both in Spanish, as it is a legal requirement, and in English, as most of our customer base is English-speaking. OK, what's next? Setting up your website. The actual mechanics of it …

6.4

Ben: … OK, what's next? Setting up your website. The actual mechanics of it. Now our website is actually hosted in the USA by a company we're very happy with. Why are we hosting our website in America and not Spain?

Marina: Well, the main reason our web host is in the USA is cos it's cheaper.

Ben: Yeah.

Marina: But also cos the service you get is better. You get more bandwidth, the customer service is quicker—

Ben: And they tend to have more up-to-date online technologies on their server. OK, let's move on to talk about getting your website designed. Marina.

Marina: We've used *Elance* for a few things. *Elance* is an online service where you can find information about the project you want to complete and people will make you offers from all around the world.

Ben: Yeah. That's E-L-A-N-C-E dot com, *elance. com*. Very useful. You outline your project, people bid, and there is a great feedback system there from people who have already used the bidders so you can decide who is going to be best for your project. We actually did all of the web design ourselves, using Open Source software. Most of our sites are based on *WordPress*, which is a free piece of software – blogging software – that is very easy to customise. Even the store software we use is free. Right, I think that's most of the main points covered. Er, finally, how about if people want a bit of inspiration? Any books or websites that they might want to look at?

Marina: There was a book called *The 4-hour Week* which gave us a lot of inspiration and ideas. Even if we don't work four hours a week.

Ben: The four-hour week is a myth. Who works only four hours a week?

Marina: Yeah. And a book—

Ben: OK, so wait, I think that's at fourhourworkweek.com or you can google Tim Ferriss, F-E-R-R-I-S-S to find the book. And a website I really like is copyblogger.com. Well, I think that's all for now. Links to everything as usual over at notesfromspain.com. See you soon. Bye

Marina: Bye bye!

7.1

Marianne: Good morning, everybody. My name is Marianne Reed, and I'm the managing director of *Media Design Advertising* here in New York. It's great to finally meet face-to-face after speaking only on the phone.

To begin with, I hope you won't mind me saying something about our history. Our headquarters are in Milan, and this is our main branch outside Italy, with 22 more scattered around the States, Australia, Japan and, of course, Europe. We have 2,300 employees altogether.

We're a very well-established company with many years of valuable experience. We've worked with many of the top names in the fashion, food and transport industries, though we specialise in media products. Over the years we've won numerous awards for our innovative approach to advertising, and just last year we won three prizes at the annual advertising media awards, both at a national level and internationally. I can honestly say that we've never had a dissatisfied client.

Well, if there are no questions…? I think we might as well get started then. I'd like to hand you over to our art director, Dave Terry.

Dave: Good morning. I'd like to start by showing you a few of the campaigns we've produced in the past couple of years, which seem to be in line with what you would like us to do for your newspaper. OK, so on the walls around this room you can see some examples of our best print ads. For instance, this is a poster for a very popular fashion magazine, while these here are some shots from an ad for a multimedia company. Many of these campaigns have won prestigious awards for outstanding design.

You'll also notice the TV screens around the room showing some of our best TV ads. Sorry the sound's turned down, but I'm sure you can see that we always go for a very powerful visual effect. The one showing right now, for instance, was for—

Marianne: Er, sorry to interrupt, Dave, but I think Cecily Valley, our copywriter, has something to add here.

Cecily: Yes, could I just say that we always adapt and translate the slogans of each ad to take into account the cultural sensitivities of the countries where the product is being launched.

Raffaella: May I just make a quick point here? I'm Raffaella Livingstone, the general account manager. I think it's important to emphasise that in the campaigns shown here, sales, according to our sales and marketing analysis, increased dramatically by up to 35% once the campaigns were launched.

Marianne: Any initial thoughts or comments, Mr McEwans?

John McEwans: There's no doubt your work is of an extremely high quality. Of course, we were aware of that before coming here, and we can see that you definitely live up to your excellent reputation. I've been a brand manager for many years, and I think those TV ads you've just shown us are really impressive. What do you think of them, Frances? My assistant brand manager, Ms Lohan, has considerable expertise in this field.

Frances Lohan: Mm, I must say the graphics are incredibly effective, and the slogans are really snappy. I think a print and TV campaign along these lines would certainly meet our objectives at *The Daily Sunshine*.

Marianne: Well, now you know who we are and what we can produce. We do hope you'll send us a full brief soon so we can prepare our proposal. How about meeting again in ten days' time, say, on 1st August?

7.2

Marianne: Good afternoon, everybody. Welcome back to *Media Design Advertising*. Needless to say, we're delighted to be chosen to handle your campaign; we'll make sure you won't regret it. Mr McEwans, if there's anything you would like to say before we proceed, please go ahead.

John: Well, as we told you in our brief, we intend to launch a brand advertising campaign in six months' time at the very latest. Our market is middle-class newspaper readers in their late twenties to early forties. Do you think you can provide us with a complete campaign by then?

Raffaella: Well, it all depends on what kind of campaign you have in mind. Just print? Or a full-range launch involving print, TV, radio and billboards?

John: Considering the budget at our disposal, which is somewhere between $800–$900,000, we're prepared to spend a third of the money on a print campaign and the rest on a prime-time TV slot.

Marianne: Well, it seems there's no time for delay then! But don't worry: we're used to working at even shorter notice.

John: How long would it take you to produce the campaign?

Marianne: Well, I think that we'll be able to do it in three to four months. Is that right, Raffaella?

Raffaella: Realistically, I'd say four months. But it all depends on the production team. It's summer, and a lot of people are away on holiday.

Marianne: Don't worry, Mr McEwans, we won't take longer than necessary. And let me add that we traditionally don't work with more than one client in any given sector, so you're guaranteed our full attention.

John: Well, that sounds both promising and professional. And what about commission?

Raffaella: If I may, we always tell our clients that what matters is not our price, but the selling power of your adverts. In any case, if it's OK with you, I'll send an email tomorrow giving you a quote and drawing together all the details of the contract, including the deadline when the campaign will be ready. And, I can assure you, Mr McEwans, we'll provide you with work of an extremely high standard, and make sure you get an unforgettable campaign.

Marianne: Also, very importantly, you'll have the opportunity to get your adverts trialled with test audiences before you pay us. That way there's no risk of you being dissatisfied with the finished product.

John: Great. In that case, you won't mind if I request that my assistant, Frances, talks to your art director in more depth about a few of our own ideas for the campaign.

Marianne: That's no problem at all. Dave will be here in a minute. Can you please tell Dave Terry to come to the meeting room immediately. Thanks. By the way, Raffaella, will you please arrange a brainstorming meeting for next week? Right, shall we …

▬▬ 7.3

Marianne: How is everyone this morning? Good, I hope. So, after a week of deep thought, what have you got? Any thoughts on the media campaign?

Dave: We've come up with a few ideas, actually. How about this picture showing all these people sitting on a bus and reading the newspaper?

Marianne: Good idea, but I've got a feeling it's been done before, hasn't it? But let's keep an open mind – I'll write it up on the board. All ideas are good ideas. What about you, Cecily? What have you come up with in the copywriting department?

Cecily: Well, I've written down a few catchy slogans, but there's the one that I like the most: "*The Daily Sunshine*: Nobody Lies in the *Sunshine*". Isn't 'truth' the main idea Mr McEwans wants to convey to his readers, together with the idea of free speech?

Dave: Mm … Yes, that's really clever. Of course, we should think of something symbolising freedom of speech, too. I tell you what, when you mentioned lying in the sun, you reminded me of my trip to Madagascar a few years ago. I was struck by the way the people gathered around baobab trees to discuss all sorts of issues. I remember its branches shooting out all over the place. I think that would make a great combination, where these branches would stand for the possibility of expressing opinions freely.

Marianne: Well, it seems like a good idea, apart from the fact that not everybody knows about Madagascar or baobab trees.

Cecily: Yes, that's true. But as you know, advertising doesn't necessarily have to convey a direct message, as long as it arouses people's curiosity. Anyway, I've heard about other African countries where baobab trees serve as a meeting place for many villages to discuss community matters, relate the news of the day, or tell stories. I think we should go for it.

Marianne: Well, if everyone agrees, let's pursue this idea. How about you, Raffaella? You're very quiet this morning. What's the matter? I guess you're thinking about the budget, aren't you?

Raffaella: Actually, yes. I just don't agree with the approach of talking about the ads first and then the budget, but apart from that …

Marianne: That's a fair point. What would you say, Dave or Cecily?

Dave: Well, why don't we limit the time of the TV campaign to 30 seconds only? Here's an idea: imagine some baobab trees in the foreground of the African savannah with the sun rising in the background, and when the sun is up in the sky, it turns into the cover of the newspaper itself, revealing the slogan you said before. Meanwhile, some classical music could give it that final touch of class. Say, for example, a bit from Dvořák's *New World Symphony*. We'd also need to come up with a voice-over, perhaps something like: 'Choice of the American people – *The Daily Sunshine* – voted paper of the year, 2008. A new dawn for journalism. Let *The Daily Sunshine* shed some light on your world.'

Raffaella: That's a fantastic idea, as long as you can manage to produce an ad like that within the budget we have. I think the client will love it!

Cecily: I think so, too.

Marianne: And so do I. OK then. Since we all agree on this idea, I think we should go for it. But please bear in mind that we need to have a pre-production meeting in a week to …

▬▬ 7.4

Marianne: Good afternoon, everyone. As most of you know, I'm Marianne Reed, managing director of *Media Design Advertising* here in New York. I'd like to thank you all for coming here today. It's a great pleasure to present this outstanding TV campaign that we've prepared for you: 'The tree of news'.

John: Thank you. We're really looking forward to seeing what you've come up with.

Marianne: Thanks, John. Let's begin by watching the advertisement … We knew that you'd like the advert. What we'd like to do now is go into the thinking behind the ad. By the way, if you have any questions, please don't hesitate to interrupt; my colleagues and I will be happy to answer them. I'm now going to hand you over to our art director, David Terry, to introduce the artistic aspect of this campaign. As you can see for yourselves, the photography is one of the strong points of this particular piece of work.

Dave: Good afternoon, everyone. I want to draw your attention to the strange beauty of this tree that we've called 'the tree of news' – a baobab tree. We hope you like the photography as much as we do: the atmospheric setting and the rising sun represent both the dawning of a new day as well as the latest news. You'll also notice that the absence of people grabs your attention. Furthermore, we believe that the use of classical music, in this case Dvořák's *New World Symphony*, underlines the fact that this is a serious newspaper. We hope the photography will be appreciated because of the contrast of colour and tone, and also because it brings out the points highlighted by the text so brilliantly. But I think my colleague Cecily can go more into that as the copywriter.

Cecily: Good afternoon, everybody. As David has just said, we've come up with a fantastic combination of words and images; something that's simple, easy to read and memorise, and, most importantly, very persuasive. Then, to

tie in perfectly with the image, we have the slogan: "*The Daily Sunshine*: Nobody Lies in the *Sunshine*". The play on words manages to convey the message that *The Daily Sunshine* is a completely reliable and honest newspaper whose journalists want to present the facts.

John: Very impressive. Everything looks great, very convincing. I do have just one little query though. Why a baobab and why is it called 'the tree of news'?

Dave: Good question! You see, baobabs are used as a meeting point in some African countries. People from many different villages meet under these trees to discuss community issues and tell the latest daily news or stories. That is what makes this ad campaign so special.

John: Indeed, well done!

Marianne: OK, enough, otherwise Dave will be asking for a huge pay raise! Well, as it seems there are no other questions, I'd suggest we move on to the print campaign.

▬▬ 8.1

Hilary: Morning, everyone. Well then, it seems we're having problems with *Sparkle*. Basically, sales are falling. Robert, please, what's the latest on this front?

Robert: As the first graph shows, there's been a dramatic 20% decline in the number of copies sold during financial year 2007/8 compared with those sold during 2006/7. Sales have dropped from 151,056 copies to 120,845—

Hilary: Sorry to interrupt, but how much is that in market share terms?

Robert: Well, this is shown in the next two graphs. Graph 2 shows that in the previous year we had around 35% of the market share with *Sparkle*, whereas our main competitor, *Golden*, had just under 50, and *Jewels* the remaining 15 or so. In Graph 3 you can see that in the past 12 months we lost 7 percentage points of our original market share altogether, while our competitors' sales have risen by 5 percentage points and 2 percentage points respectively.

▬▬ 8.2

Hilary: Do we know what's caused this decline in sales?

Robert: Well, it seems that *Sparkle* is simply no longer appealing to readers between 25 and 35. We've virtually lost contact with that market segment. Obviously the problem is with the product itself and to some extent with promotion. We need to raise brand awareness.

Frank: This is all pretty bad, isn't it?

Robert: Well, it's certainly not great news, no. But we can reverse this negative trend if we look carefully at the four Ps to see where we can increase demand. I'm sure that if we can get the marketing mix right, we'll get our customers back.

Hilary: Thanks, Robert. Now, I saw these figures when the analysis came in last week, and I've been thinking about what we should do. Here's what I've come up with. We need to take immediate action by setting new objectives. We also need to take into account the findings from the competitor analysis and the trend report which were presented to us last week. I also think we need to redesign our overall communication strategy. Any ideas on how we can do that, Maggie?

Maggie: Um, I suppose the first thing we should do is increase consumer awareness of *Sparkle* and reinforce its image as one of the most contemporary, prestigious and exclusive magazines on the market.

Frank: Yes.

Maggie: Secondly, we should investigate new communication tools so we can create marketing material that addresses customers' needs. Integrated marketing communications. That's the solution to the problem – good old IMC.

Robert: Um, talking about needs, one extremely important finding that emerged from our marketing analysis is that younger people are strongly attracted to digital magazines.

Frank: You mean online magazines, don't you?

Robert: Yeah, it's the same thing. Our problem is that our competitors have invested a lot of time and money in digital magazines and managed to broaden their readership.

▬ 8.3

Hilary: Yes. In fact, it all links up with my idea that *Sparkle* badly needs restyling. I think we could improve results by using more creative and original photos. That means hiring the best photographers on the market. We also need a graphic layout that's more contemporary and functional, and perhaps even a more appealing font.

Maggie: Absolutely. We should also bring in a fashion consultant.

Frank: Um, but it would be great if we could also have an advertising campaign, wouldn't it?

Hilary: Yes, it would. But, as always, it depends on the budget. In any case, when we know the answer to that we'll need to come up with a coherent strategy and decide what to do, and who's going to do it. It goes without saying that a key role will be played by the PR and the press office. And this is where both of you, Maggie and Frank, with your teams, can do a lot to get us out of this difficult situation.

Maggie: I hope so. You're suggesting not only a complete restyling, but also the inclusion of new content, aren't you?

Hilary: That's right. I believe that both of these ingredients will increase our readership and give a big boost to our sales. We need to relaunch *Sparkle* as soon as possible. You should start setting up the communication strategy and activity scheduling as soon as you can. Today is February the 7th … I guess one week will be enough for the communication strategy, won't it?

Maggie: I'd think so. Frank?

Frank: Yes, that seems realistic.

Hilary: Right then, I'll get some costs for these objectives we've discussed. I'll email you with that information well before our next meeting. If everything goes according to plan, I would expect the launch to take place in eight months, just in time to catch the September issue. Any questions or comments? No? OK, that's it for today then. Oh, Jennifer, please, don't forget to email me the minutes of this meeting. I need them on my desk by 10 o'clock tomorrow morning, as I have to brief the chief executive officer.

▬ 8.4

Hilary: Hello, everyone. Well, the atmosphere seems a bit more relaxed this week. That's a good sign! Now, Maggie, before you update us on the activity scheduling and the promotion action plan, I've got some good news. Another project has been cancelled in order to make more money available for *Sparkle*. So I can now confirm that *Sparkle*'s relaunch will include an advertising campaign. We hope this will involve the endorsement of actresses Claudia Schneider and Nicole Lopez, who will appear both in the press and on TV. In light of that, and the activities run by your department, the great news is that a generous budget of two million dollars has been set.

Maggie: Wow!

Frank: That's fantastic news!

Hilary: Of course, you're aware we'll need to create a synergy between the advertising campaign and all the other communication channels we plan to use. Anyway, I trust you've managed to produce something as good as you always do.

Maggie: I hope so. Anyway, it's great that they've approved the advertising campaign. It'll help to maximise visibility in the media. Frank will talk us through the action plan we've put together.

▬ 8.5

Frank: Well, if we confirm that the launch is to be held on September 5, we need to move quickly to organise an outstanding international event on the same date. The event will be for our biggest advertisers, the managing directors of top jewellery brands, and of course celebrities. We'll have to send the invitations by July in order to make sure that they attend. We'll also need to create a press kit for the event, including a press release, the September cover and a CD containing the visuals of the advertising campaign.

Jennifer: Um, sorry to interrupt, but we've just received news from Claudia Schneider and Nicole Lopez for the celebrity endorsement. It looks likely we'll be able to get both of them.

Frank: Wow!

Maggie: That's great. Our idea is to have them photographed while reading *Sparkle*. As soon as they're 100% confirmed, we'll fix a date for the shoot.

Hilary: Sounds great. But it's also really important that we get some positive articles written about the relaunch. So to start with, I assume you're planning to invite the chief editors of other *Canada Media* magazines to the event, along with sponsors and investors? Also, what are our chances of getting some product placement opportunities in the future?

Maggie: Um, I think we could. In the meantime, we need to start generating some excitement about the event. We'll have to send the celebrities a save-the-date by March. The location, as well as the celebrities attending, will be extremely important if we want to make sure that the top journalists in the luxury field cover the event. Concerning the placement of *Sparkle* in movies, I've already briefed the placement agency. In a few weeks we should receive some production proposals to evaluate. It would be fantastic if we could get our magazine to appear in a blockbuster movie next fall.

▬ 8.6

Hilary: It all sounds extremely positive. However, our market analyst, Robert Vaughan, has told us that another decision was made during the recent meeting at the CEO's office. Management have agreed that if we want to increase our market to include a younger demographic age group, we should really expand our online presence. So they have set aside a significant amount of money to do this. We're going to have an improved browsable online version of the magazine. That means we can establish an interactive relationship not only with our readers but also among our readers. This will provide a unique social networking facility and feedback system.

Maggie: That's excellent news. We can include an information sheet on that in the press kit. I'm sure our potential younger readers will be very interested to hear about it.

Hilary: Right. People who read the magazine online aren't only interested in the product but are also prepared to interact with the company. This is where our direct competitors are – sorry, 'were' – way ahead of us, as shown by their good results.

Frank: Too true.

Hilary: Yes, the whole thing sounds fantastic. I think we're on the right track. Unless anyone has anything else to add, I think that's it.

▬ 8.7

Maggie: Hi, Frank! Great news: it seems we're nearly there. Only a few more major deadlines. We'll probably only need to meet a couple more times before we finish.

Frank: That's good. It's been quite stressful trying to keep working at this rate. I think the whole team's really starting to feel it. Anyway, here are the last proofs of the material for the press kit; we need to get the green light on them ASAP in order to meet the final deadline.

Maggie: I'm sure you're doing an excellent job with the press kit.

Frank: Thanks. By the way, what do you think of this slogan on the front of the invitation cards for the launch event here in Vancouver: 'At last, sophisticated women get the magazine they've always deserved'?

Maggie: Excellent!

Frank: And I'd like your opinion on something else, too. After a careful and lengthy selection process, we've received these three photos to choose from for the covers of the September issue of our magazine.

Maggie: Let me see. All of them look good. But wow, this one with the woman holding the rose seems to be exactly what we're looking for. An image like this should help us to attract both the younger and more mature market. It also gives the magazine an air of elegance and refinement. I'd go for this one.

Frank: OK. Good choice.

Maggie: Great job! And have you completed the final arrangements for the launch event yet?

Frank: Yes. The main advertisers and the top press people have already been contacted and most have confirmed they're coming. As usual, getting the testimonials that we need from the celebrities is more difficult, but that's normal, so don't worry. I'll make sure a few celebrities will come anyway, as that'll help get the press to attend as well.

Maggie: Well done to you and all of your team. I'm really impressed with the way you've organised the event. That's brilliant work. Well, the end is in sight. Um, just one more thing, what's the news from New York about the organisation of their local event?

Frank: Everything's fine, I spoke to …

▰ 8.8

Hilary: It was a year ago that we first met to discuss the continuing decrease in *Sparkle*'s readership, and four months have passed since the relaunch. The purpose of this meeting is to analyse the success of our relaunch plan, and the effect it's having on our sales. Maggie, would you like to start?

Maggie: OK. Our efforts have been very successful in general. To start with, here are some key figures about the event we organised to relaunch *Sparkle*: there were 320 attendees, 185 press kits were distributed, and the press coverage was positive in the two weeks following the September issue.

Frank: There's no doubt that the restyled version of *Sparkle* has been a hit. The feedback we've received from advertisers so far is very encouraging, while the advertising revenue from selling space in the magazine has been very good so far.

Hilary: Well, it's clear that we've managed to reverse the trend. As a matter of fact, according to the latest report I received this morning from the Marketing Analysis department, *Sparkle*'s print run has been gradually increasing. Over the past four months, we've seen a 4% gain in copies sold. This also means we've regained 1.12 percentage points of the market share we lost, putting us at 29.12%. All the more reason to propose a toast to the new improved *Sparkle* and to continued increasing sales.

ANSWER KEY

■ Unit 1

1c
2 e   3 g   4 b   5 h   6 c
7 f   8 a

d
'When?' and 'Why?' questions cannot usually be answered: 'When?' because it is often something that has happened recently; 'Why?' because the answer will usually be found in the article.

f
1 Articles, auxiliary verbs, pronouns
2 Present simple for recent events, to + infinitive to describe future events, past participle for passive constructions
3 Abbreviations, exclamation marks

2a
2 Change of tense (present perfect to present simple), omission of relative pronoun and verb
3 Punctuation changed, omission of verb and auxiliary verbs
4 Change to passive voice, omission of subject (the judge), omission of articles

b
Suggested answers
1 Rare bird returns to UK after 400 years
2 Drunk driver kills 2
3 Australian PM to open hospital in Melbourne

3a
Cultural references: *Choose That Girl! Madge jets to Africa to adopt girl* (Madonna had a song called *Who's that girl?*)
Alliteration: *Love's Labour's Lost*
Emphatic language: *Family's pet dog butchered* (butchered = killed brutally)

b
Suggested answers
Tabloids: *The Sun, The Star, The Daily Mirror, The Daily Mail, The Daily Express, New York Post, Boston Herald*
Broadsheets: *The Times, The Guardian, The Independent, The Daily Telegraph, The Observer, The New York Times, The Washington Post, The Wall Street Journal*
Note: the words 'tabloid' and 'broadsheet' originally referred to the size of the newspaper; tabloids were smaller, and broadsheets larger. Now, however, the word is often used to denote the 'quality' of the news, especially in the British press; tabloids are more interested in gossip, sport and 'celebrity news', whereas broadsheets give more analysis and coverage to international and national news. However, some well-known broadsheets, such as *The Times* and *The Guardian,* are now the same size as tabloids.

c
1 c   2 e   3 a   4 b   5 d

d
1 Play on words (Titanic disaster = very large disaster; *Titanic* disaster = the disaster when the Titanic sank)
2 Cultural reference (*To be or not to be* is a famous line from Shakespeare's *Hamlet*)
3 Alliteration (*Gorgeous George – Clooney conquers Cannes*)
4 Emphatic language (carnage = the violent killing of large numbers of people, especially in war)
5 Tabloidese (axe = cut)

4c
1 conservative, reactionary, emotive
2 liberal, neutral

d
Emotive: muggers, yobs, fed up with, terrorise, discrimination, crime epidemic, low-level disorder, outsider, intimidated
Neutral: teenagers, ban, weapon, shoplifting, law-abiding

e
1 A   2 B

f
Article A does not mention the topic.
Article B asks questions.

h
Young people
Article A: young people, teenagers
Article B: child, children, teenagers, kids, youth
Crime
Article A: thugs, muggers, yobs, law-abiding citizens, robberies, gangster-style, armed robberies, shoplifting, intimidation, commit crime, terrorise victims
Article B: yobbishness, low-level disorder, victims, attackers

Article A has few references to young people but lots to crime, whereas Article B has more references to young people and much fewer to crime. In Article A, the journalist also avoids the use of the word 'child', suggesting that we shouldn't treat hoodies as children. In Article B, the use of 'child' has the opposite effect – it allows us to look at hoodies not as dangerous adults but as young children. The choice of words associated with crime in Article A is also interesting: emotive, emphatic terms like 'gangster-style', 'yob' and 'terrorise' create a sense that hoodies are responsible for serious, violent crime. In Article B, the use of the term 'low-level disorder' suggests the opposite – that the types of crime committed by hoodies are not too serious at all.

i
1 F   2 F   3 T   4 T   5 T
6 F

5a
1 c   2 b   3 d   4 a

b
1 <u>They</u> behave as if <u>they</u> own the streets …
2 <u>They</u> are the uniform of <u>thugs</u> and <u>muggers</u> …
3 <u>So</u> the decision by Bluewater shopping centre in Kent to ban the clothing …
4 … the hoodie has become a symbol for <u>those</u> we fear have taken control.

c
<u>They</u> (CCTV cameras) record crimes as <u>they</u> (crimes) are happening but do not prevent <u>them</u> (crimes) happening. In such an environment there is a feeling that the streets and town centres do not properly belong to <u>us</u> (the reader / 'ordinary people') and the hoodie has become a symbol for <u>those</u> (people) <u>we</u> (the reader / 'ordinary people') fear have taken control.

d
1 Passive
2 The first sentence uses the passive to create cohesion. The second sentence uses the passive to avoid mentioning who does the action.

e
have been adopted (to avoid mentioning subject), *they should be allowed* (to avoid mentioning subject and to create cohesion), *are carried out* (to avoid mentioning subject), *have been bought* (to avoid mentioning subject)

6b
She talks about her education and her past and present jobs.

c
1 F   2 T   3 T   4 T

d
2 reporter
3 editor
4 education
5 deputy
6 Afternoon
7 press
8 circulation
9 diversify
10 camcorders
11 digital
12 foreign

f
2 Did you enjoy the positions?
3 Will you continue as head of the press office?
4 Are you looking for a new position?
5 Have newspapers changed during your career?
6 How would you describe the present newspaper market in the UK?
7 Is the era of print newspapers coming to an end?
8 Who is your media inspiration?
9 Do you have any advice for people … ?

g
3 a –   b Will   c you   d continue
  e as head of the press office?
4 a –   b Are   c you   d looking for
  e a new position?
5 a –   b Have   c newspapers
  d changed   e during your career?
6 a How   b would c you   d describe
  e the present newspaper market in the UK?
7 a –   b Is   c the era of print newspapers
  d coming   e to an end?
8 a Who b is   c your media inspiration
  d –   e – ?
9 a –   b Do   c you   d have
  e any advice for people … ?

h
Introductions
How do you do?
Nice to meet you.
I'm …
Pleased to meet you.

Interrupting
Hold on, …
Could I just say something?
Sorry, but …
Can I interrupt for a moment?

Hang on a minute, …
Sorry to interrupt, but …
Sorry to butt in (again) …

Hesitating
Well …
You know …
I mean …
So …
Right …
OK …

Asking for detail
What exactly do you mean?
What exactly were they?
Could you be more specific?
Why do you say that?

8a
Suggested answers
Abbreviations, accents, capitals, italics, plurals, titles, etc.

c
Suggested answers
1   Yes, inconsistency is distracting.
2   No, 'style' in the sense of 'house style' does not refer to a stylish appearance or design.
3   Yes, readers get used to a house style and identify with it.

d

House style feature	*Daily Mail* house style	Alternative house style
Punctuation	" "	' '
Spelling	realised	realized
Capitalisation	Prime Minister	prime minister
Foreign words	cafe	café
Use of American/ British/ Australian English	shopping centre	shopping mall

9a
1   Brainstorm the topic (write down ideas connected to the article)
2   Research the story
3   Plan (organise and paragraph your ideas)
4   Write the introduction
5   Write the main body of the article
6   Conclude
7   Check your article for mistakes

b
The article is about a safe which has been stolen from a kindergarten in Ipswich.

c
The headline tells us 'who': a group of people (*a gang*) and 'how': through a hole in the wall.

e
1   Doesn't say exactly where, when and how.
2   Time vague, doesn't say who the victims were, and it introduces irrelevant information.
3   **The best option**: it answers who, where, what, and how.

f
1   Journalist's opinion is too obviously stated.
2   **The best option**: the headlines and photos are now more fully explained, using the words of the victim. Use of police quotation to reassure the public.
3   The message is the same as (2), but is less interesting to read as it doesn't contain any direct quotations.

■■■ Unit 2

1c
2 e   3 a   4 f   5 d   6 b

d
2   News and sport
3   News and current affairs
4   Classical, jazz and world music
5   News and sport
6   Classical, jazz and world music
7   Global news and documentary
8   Popular music

e
Introducing the show/presenter/DJ
It's 6 o'clock on Monday 24th September. This is *The Morning Show* with John Gray in London …
It's 8 o'clock, and you're having breakfast with me, Amanda Green.
And now it's time for *Everyday Women* … with Carla Morris.
I'm Gemma Wilson and welcome to *In Focus*.
I'm Mo Ace and this is a free podcast.
Introducing guests/ features/news
Let's talk to Jonathon White, our football correspondent.
We'll be speaking to the Prime Minister at ten past eight.
Now over to the newsroom.
This week, Rahim Anwar presents a programme about the poet Auden …
Introducing music
We've still got Madonna's *Ray Of Light* to play for you, and a track from The Beatles, but first, The Foo Fighters' *Learn To Fly*.
Here's the second movement of Beethoven's *Emperor Concerto*, performed by the Berlin Philharmonic Orchestra and conducted by Heinrich Erhard.

f
1   You're listening **to** Radio Australia. I'm Gil Brennen and welcome **to** *Good Morning Australia*.
2   Here's Bach's Concerto for keyboard in D major, performed **by** Alison Balsom and Colm Carey.
3   It's Tuesday the 19th January. This is *Report*, with Bill Noles and Justine Welsh. Still to come in the next half hour, we'll be interviewing **to** Janie Kirk.
4   That was Coldplay **with** *Viva la vida*, Before that, you heard *Rockstar* **by** Nickelback.
5   This week, John Walsh presents a programme **about** finding work on the Internet.

2b
1   In many ways, a radio commissioning brief is like a job advertisement: it describes a product/service that a person/company wants to be provided with; in this case, London 1 is looking for producers to make documentaries.
2   Somebody in London 1's commissioning team.
3   People, most likely producers, who want to and are able to produce short radio documentaries.
4   This document was taken from the London 1 website; another place to find briefs such as this would be in trade papers.

c
1   Young people (the under-25s)
2   Two selected highlights, a dry version for podcasting, a piece of visual to be placed on the website for viral marketing.
3   Three
4   Documentaries on music, youth and social issues

5   One sends producers to the editorial guidelines; the other gives details of additional requirements (cues, billings, etc.).
6   £3,000
7   Midnight, 16 May
8   From August until early next year

d
2   format   6   key audience
3   podcast   7   trail ahead
4   dry version   8   go on air
5   cues   9   viral marketing

3c
2   running order   7   packages
3   breaking news   8   stringer
4   lead stories   9   debriefing
5   to brief   10   to update
6   news list   11   to liaise

d
debriefing: to debrief
shortlist: to shortlist
package: to package

e
2   shortlist   7   brief
3   stringer   8   breaking news
4   running order   9   Update
5   lead stories   10   Liaise
6   packages   11   Debriefing

g
editor, deputy editor, reporter, researcher, producer, journalist, presenter, guest, studio manager

4a
1   Rising house prices   3   A new museum
2   Schools closing   4   Global warming

b
Can/could you deal with … ?
I want you to …
I'd like (an) …
I'd like you to …
Speak to …
Contact …
You'll need to …
Do you mean … ?
Should I … ?

c
A: Giving instructions
B: Checking instructions

d
The most direct are the imperatives (*Speak to …* , *Use …* , *Contact …*). If not used in an appropriate situation or with appropriate intonation, direct instructions using the imperative can seem rude. The most indirect is *Would you mind … ?* This makes the instruction seem more polite.

e
+ noun or person
Can/could you deal with …
I'd like (an) …
Speak to …
Do you mean … ? (can also be followed by a clause)
Use …
Contact …

+ gerund
Would you mind … ?

+ infinitive
I want you to …
I'd like you to …
Will you … ?
You'll need to …
Shall I … ?
Should I … ?

f

1 Shall I **to** use our contacts database?
2 I'd like a five-minute package on that story.
3 I'd like you **to brief** the guests thoroughly.
4 I want you **to** liaise with our stringer in San Francisco.
5 **Would** you mind checking the story for accuracy?

5b

estate agent / house prices
schools / birth rate
global warming / overhyped
names / cruelty
honour / World War II
museum / homeless shelter

e

1 T
2 T
3 F – but controversial news is often more likely to be reported; item 5 in the news list is not particularly controversial but has an important element of emotional/human interest.
4 T – sentences 1–5 use either the present simple or the present continuous. Even finished events such as item 6 are reported in the present perfect to make them seem more immediate and of the moment. However, other verb forms can be used when relevant, for example *will* for future events.
5 F – they can be questions.

f

1 Is the Liberal Party leader too old to win the general election?
2 Top universities are still failing to attract large numbers of students from state schools.
3 It's Oscar time again, but are the Oscars valid, or just another marketing ploy?

g

1 Explaining how to develop the story
2 The imperative
3 Because she is giving instructions and wants to give a sense of urgency; it is also the shortest way of expressing what she wants done.

6a

Write – script, interview questions for guests
People to interview – someone representing the museum, someone representing the homeless people
Fee – standard fee
Deadline – 4 pm Australian time

b

2 want
3 You'll also need
4 They'll be needed
5 Can
6 will be
7 need
8 We'll need

The meanings of the sentences in Exercise 6b are very similar, regardless of which alternative word is used, but note the following points:
• *Will* can make demands seem less direct.
• *Can* is sometimes more direct than *could*.
• *As* is more common in written language; *because* or *'cos* are more common in spoken language.
• *Need* is more urgent than *want*.

7b

Research not done well – N
Being first with breaking news – P
Studio going down for several seconds – N
Getting an eyewitness report for a breaking news story – P
Interviewees not briefed well – N

c

A booked speaker does not arrive for the show
Studio going down for several seconds
Getting an eyewitness report for a breaking news story

d

2 great moment
3 what happened
4 cause was; happening again
5 happened to
6 account; real
7 happy with; well done

8a

1 understand = figure out
   stop working = go down
2 They are both phrasal verbs.

b

1 T
2 F – the meaning is sometimes literal (for example, *sit down*) but in other cases, as in the examples in Exercise 8a, the meaning is non-literal.
3 F – some phrasal verbs have only one meaning (for example, *sit down*) but many phrasal verbs have several different meanings.
4 T

c

1 Moving on
2 Coming up; go over
3 lined up
4 wind up; run out of

d

2 tuned in
3 make up; get away with
4 set aside
5 do without

9a

The studio going down, the meteorologist not turning up, the eyewitness account of the rail crash, and the stringer in France

b

1 Yes
2 Yes, with reference to the meteorology expert. Also implicit is the fact that Dawn would have liked to break the news of the rail crash.
3 At the beginning of the email there is no salutation; Dawn instead chooses to thank the staff for their work. To finish, she simply puts her name.
4 *Starting with the bad news* + clause
   Unfortunately + clause
   On a positive note + clause
5 Relatively informal but still authoritative (see answer 3 above). The email uses standard English, but note the use of dashes, an exclamation mark, contractions, and a sentence beginning with *and*, all of which are more typical of informal communication.

Unit 3

1c

Title: *Glorious*
Price: £3.75
Issue number: 8
Date: January 2009
Bar code: in the bottom right-hand corner
Coverline: There's never a dull moment!

e

1 House Beautiful, Beautiful Britain, Simply Knitting, What Car?, PS3
2 Vogue, Cosmopolitan, Esquire, Glamour
3 GQ, FHM, T3

2a

1 a or b	5 e	
2 a	6 a or b	
3 c	7 a or b	
4 a or d	8 a	

c

1 c   2 a   3 b   4 e   5 d

d

1 font style, capitalisation, colour
2 font style, colour
3 font style, question, imperative, underlining
4 quotation
5 font style, colour
6 colour

3a

A women's magazine

b

1 a   2 b

c

1 rhyming
2 alliteration
3 alliteration
4 rhyming and alliteration
5 alliteration
6 rhyming
7 alliteration

e/f

Suggested answers

2 Jen and Paul. It's getting serious! "She's fantastic!" he says
3 Stunning garden makeover! (It's easier than you think!)
4 The hottest new diet – lose ten kilos in two months!
5 Get fit and quit – how exercise can help you give up nicotine
6 This year's coolest new cars
7 The greatest guitar tracks ever!

4a

Suggested answers

Celebrity news and interviews, romance, fashion, beauty, health, food, money, work and careers, reviews, horoscopes, homes and interior design, shopping, true life, personal problems

b

Food, fashion, true-life stories, romance

c

1 New designers in Rio
2 Vegetarian food
3 Because she has to leave suddenly to take an urgent call
4 Beach destinations in Rio
5 Commissioning articles, April 21st; copy, May 19th; artwork, May 30th
6 Thursday at 10 am

d

According to the fashion editor, who <u>are going to be</u> big names in the future?

Why does the editor in chief say "<u>I'll hand</u> you over to Richard."?

What <u>is</u> Grace <u>going to do</u> a short piece about?

When <u>are</u> the deadlines for commissioning articles, copy and artwork?

When <u>are</u> the members of the editorial team <u>meeting</u> to make the final decision on contents for the July issue?

1 To express a spontaneous decision about the future: *will*
2 To talk about a plan for the future made before the moment of speaking: *be going to*
3 To talk about a fixed future arrangement: present continuous (*are meeting*)
4 To talk about a future schedule: present simple (*are*)
5 To make a prediction about the future: *be going to* (*will* can also be used for future predictions)

e
1 Beauty editor
2 Could be all of them, but probably the picture editor
3 Deputy editor
4 All of them
5 Fashion editor or deputy editor

f
1 *will*, spontaneous decision about the future
2 present continuous, fixed future arrangement
3 *be going to*, plan for the future made before the moment of speaking
4 *be going to*, prediction about the future
5 present simple, future schedule

g
1 'm interviewing
2 's
3 'll proofread
4 'm going to be paid

5a

Making and justifying a proposal
I'd like to propose a piece on … , as …
It might be expensive, but …

Making objections
I don't know.

Dealing with objections
That's not a problem.

d
1 c   2 a   3 b   4 c

e

Keeping order
Let's get back to the point.

Handing over
I'll hand you over to Richard.

Summing up
Let's go over what we've decided so far.
Have I covered everything?

6b
1 Yes. They both refer to the possibility of work on the photo shoot in Rio, and Charlotte asks the photographer to contact her for more information if he is interested in the job.
2 Email B is more informal. Email A has a more formal salutation and ending; it is written using *we* not *I* (*we* referring to companies, rather than *I* which refers to individual people); it uses conditional forms; it does not contain any chatty small talk, abbreviations, or other informal language.

c
3 Always   7 Never
4 Always   8 Never
5 Never   9 Never
6 Always

d
Both the emails follow the rules.

e
2 Informal (e.g. *I'm, I've, I'll*)
3 Formal
4 Informal (e.g. *Working hard?* instead of *Are you working hard?*)
5 Informal (e.g. *ASAP, re*)

7b
The first message is more formal. She uses her full name, including surname, and makes a polite request using *could*. She also finishes the message by saying *thank you*. In the second message, she only uses her first name, uses an imperative to make a request (*give me a ring*), and ends the call with the more informal sign-off *speak to you soon*.

c
1 b get back to you   c This is d ring me back on
2 a Leave me a message   b It's   c ring

8b
1 Fee   4 Contact
2 Timescale   5 Brief
3 Context

c
1 a   2 a   3 b   4 b

9a

Suggested answer
1 True stories appear in many different types of magazine but tend to be more common in women's magazines or magazines aimed at the mass market (TV magazines, celebrity magazines, etc.).

b
1 c   2 b   3 d   4 a
Note: This is not a fixed rule and can be quite fluid. For example, there might be more than one setting, and the moral can recur throughout the text. However, it provides a basic structure.

c
1 c, d, f   3 e
2 a   4 b

10b
1 Ann Storm **felt** nervous at work.
2 Matt **was waiting** for her, his eyes full of tears.
3 Matt **managed** to say, "I need a liver transplant."
4 A donor liver **became** available.
5 Tests showed Ann **had suffered** liver failure.
6 Now it **was** Ann's turn to wait for a donor liver.
7 The operation **finished** at seven the next morning. She **left** the hospital after ten days.
8 Ann **puts** on her coat, and Matt **puts** his arm around her.

c
Past simple: sentences 1, 3, 7
Past continuous: sentence 2
Past perfect: sentence 5

d
The operation <u>went</u> well, and he <u>was</u> soon back at home. Four months after the transplant, Matt <u>was begging</u> to return to work. He <u>had read</u> 36 books and <u>(had) watched</u> every programme on TV. "I had more energy than ever," he remembers. "Life was looking good again." Then, two years later, Ann suddenly <u>fainted</u> at work. She was taken to hospital, where tests showed Ann <u>had suffered</u> liver failure. A brutally honest doctor said that Ann <u>could</u> die at any time.

e
2 say   5 explains
3 responded   6 adds
4 told

g
Remember, wonder

h
1 can/~~cannot~~
2 *Tell*/~~Say~~
3 ~~Tell~~/*Say*

i
1 added/explained   3 told
2 said/explained   4 said/explained

Unit 4

1a

Suggested answers
3 The director of news and current affairs is responsible for the gathering and production of national daily news, as well as business, political and current affairs programmes. The director of news reports to the director-general and the deputy director-general. The editor is the artistic force behind a series in TV and radio. S/he is responsible for the programme and the team, appoints and/or supervises staff, decides who does what on the programme, gives them advice and supervises them on their work, and gives feedback on their performance. Finally, s/he may change the agenda and tone of a programme. (Note that the output editor is usually responsible for one edition of a programme.)
A social affairs correspondent reports news on social affairs, for example health, drugs, population, migration, and labour and employment.
A reporter is a person who collects and reports news for a TV station.
A researcher is the person in charge of finding out facts and information about a given subject.
4 Both newspaper journalists and TV journalists collect and write news stories, for newspapers and television respectively. However, whereas the TV journalist can count on the images being shown as well as a comment being broadcast, the paper journalist has to describe things in detail to make readers visualise what's happening (although the article may also include visuals such as photos or illustrations).

b
Terrorism, trafficking, First Minister's Questions in the Scottish Parliament and floods in Bangladesh

c
1 T
2 F – s/he is in Bangladesh
3 F – the building was in Birmingham
4 T
5 T
6 F – at 2.30

d
2 d   3 e   4 a   5 g   6 c
7 b

Column 1

e

2 b	3 a	4 c	5 b	6 c
7 c	8 a			

2a

1   People who are in the production team: editor, reporter, camera operator, researcher
2   It puts together a documentary film, TV show, etc.

b

Research, interviews, filming

c

2	primary	5	talking heads
3	archives	6	viewpoint
4	brief		

d

Possibility
could

Ability
can

Giving advice/recommendation
should
had better

Necessary
must
have to
need to

Not necessary
don't have to

e

2 must ~~to~~	4 ~~need~~ needs to
3 ~~has~~ had better	5 might ~~to~~

3a

2   The editor is responsible for a programme or series as a whole. S/he takes care of organising a series of 'recces' (reconnoitres – that is, obtaining information about the shooting location). S/he also keeps a close eye on programme budgets to make sure that there is no overspending.
The production manager makes sure the equipment is working, looks into the availability of health services for the crew and other facilities (for example, a changing room, etc.).
3   Exact numbers vary, but at least the editor, reporter, camera crew and fixer.
4   It is a key element during the production phase. If all the relevant information concerning the schedule is gathered together, it makes it easier for the crew members to keep in contact with each other and with the production staff back home.

b

1   Seven days
2   At various locations in Lindovia
3   A girl who is suing her traffickers, victims of trafficking, a psychologist, representatives from the *Men Alone* organisation and the *International Organisation for Migration* (IOM).

c

1   Probably a researcher for *SBC*
2   Crew on location
3   Factual, informative
4   Infinitive without *to*

d

2	PTC	5	IV
3	TX date	6	GVs
4	R/V	7	SCU

Column 2

e

2   release forms
3   digital MP3 recorder
4   daily rates
5   digibeta
6   tape stock
7   sequences
8   carnets

f

1	release forms	3	carnets
2	daily rates	4	tape stock

g

1	R/V	5	R/V/IV
2	Get	6	R/V/IV
3	R/V/IV	7	Travel
4	Film		

4b

The sequence of shots taken
The border guards' change of attitude
The place where Neil is going to read his script

c

2	pan	6	POV
3	tracking shot	7	pull focus
4	walkie-talkie	8	personal mic
5	tilt		

5a

Saying what needs to be done
We'll need to get the guards to hold the traffic …
We might need to put the big windshield on it.
We'll give it a go and see what the sound's like.

Asking for and making suggestions
… I think we should get down to the PTC now.
I think it'd be good to have you doing a walkie-talkie.
What do you think?
If you have a better idea, please tell us.

Asking someone to do something
… could you tell the guards what we want to do, please?

6a

Generally speaking, the output editor is responsible for one edition of a programme; the editor is responsible for the whole programme or series over a longer period of time.

b

1   Because she is going to arrive late at the editing studio.
2   Diana is the output editor.
3   She may be slightly worried that Donna – who, as editor, is in charge of deciding what should be included in the documentary – won't be there at the start of the editing process. She may also be worried that a different reporter, Sylvana Calpepper, is going to have to do the voice recording because the reporter who was on the shoot, Neil, is ill. However, Donna's email is very apologetic and clearly lays out what she needs to do.

c

2   lay down
3   royalty-free compilation CD
4   EDL
5   intercut
6   shot list

d

1   can
2   the imperative
3   friendly

7a

a   Yes, she is.
b   Because he has a work commitment in Liverpool.

Column 3

b

2	booth	5	script
3	time code	6	reconstruction
4	clipspotter		

c

2 d	3 e	4 a	5 c	6 b

▓▓▓ Unit 5

1b

2	screenplay	6	special effects
3	screenwriter	7	soundtrack
4	the cast	8	the stars
5	plot	9	director

2a

1 c	2 a	3 b

3a

1   **Who?** Kaufman, a screenwriter, and Valerie, from the context a film agent
2   **Where?** In a business lunch restaurant in Los Angeles
3   **When?** Midday
4   **What?** They're having lunch.
5   **Why?** To discuss the screen adaptation of the novel *The Orchid Thief*
6   **How?** Kaufman feels hot, sweaty, self-conscious and embarrassed. Valerie, in comparison, is calm and collected, whilst being kind and encouraging to Kaufman.

b

1   No. Valerie wants to turn it into a love story, but Kaufman doesn't think it would be realistic.
2   He means a typical Hollywood film with a predictable and happy ending, without anything too strange happening.
3   For more information about the film, search the Web for *Adaptation*.

c

2	centre	5	dialogue
3	action	6	present
4	brackets	7	V.O.; INT.

d

McKee is a screenwriter who runs training seminars.

f

Incomplete sentences: *You promise?*
Missing a subject: *Tell you a secret.*
Repetition: *My brother did. My twin brother, Donald.*
Short sentences: most of the sentences in the two scenes are quite short
Simple linking words: *but, and*
Use of shared knowledge to leave things unsaid: *wow them* (i.e. the audience) *at the end*

g

Suggested answers
Other typical features of conversation include: off-topic comments, interruptions, grammatical inaccuracy, use of stress rhythm and intonation to convey meaning, rephrasing, hesitation, inviting comment

4a

1   Getting funding or selling your screenplay – that is, pitching your screenplay to film executives, producers, backers, studios, etc.

b

It is a letter asking a producer / production company to read your screenplay.

d
1 T
2 T
3 F – the tenses are either the present or *will* (not *might*).
4 T
5 F – there are no contractions or slang, and formal greetings and salutations are used.

5a
1 A *pitch* is when a screenwriter meets film executives, etc. to present his or her script. The screenwriter has a short time in which to try and sell the script.

b
1 He is the person leading the seminar, so probably an expert in screenwriting and pitching.
2 Aspiring screenwriters
3 People interested in investing in films
4 One or two minutes
5 Before the seminar
6 It is recommended that the people attending the seminar practise their pitch with their family and friends.
7 Any situation where you may have to speak in public, for example at meetings; any situation where you are expected to sell an idea or convince potential buyers of a product or service

c
1 genre   3 logline
2 title   4 hooks

d
1 b   2 c   3 a

e
1 It is an extremely short description, consisting of one or two sentences, of the general idea of the story; it is the principal aim of the story that the writer wants to convey to the audience. (Note that a *logline* is not the same as a *tagline*, which is a phrase that can accompany a film when it is released; for example, the tagline to the film *Shrek* was "The greatest fairy tale never told.")
2 It can help the screenwriter clarify his/her ideas; it gives film executives an instant idea of what the film is about.

f
1 *The Shakespeare Code*
2 *Conviction*
3 *on stAGE*

6a
1 *on stAGE*
2 Music, location, cast, target audience

b
Small talk
I trust you had no problem getting here?
So, is this your first screenplay?

The pitch
My film's called …
It's a (touching musical comedy) set in …
This film is aimed at …
There are a number of great …
(*on stAGE*) is a feelgood film …
Think (*Spinal Tap*) meets (*The Breakfast Club*).

Clarifying information about the pitch
… could you explain how the audience is expected to believe that … ?

Ending the pitch meeting
If you leave a copy with us, we'll get back to you within …

7a
Suggested answer
2 The film producer provides and controls the budget and may have a say in marketing, too. There are also producers who are more hands-on and like to take part in the director's creative role, too.
The film director's role is fundamental the whole way through production. During the pre-production phase, s/he is responsible for casting the actors and technical crews and finding locations for the shooting. During production, directors supervise the creative aspects of the film (for example, actors' rehearsals) and the technical ones (for example, the camera and sound teams' work). In short, they make sure the written film script is rendered effectively onto the screen. During post-production, s/he works closely with editors in selecting shots and editing. A good director needs to have a wide creative vision to produce an original and involving film. S/he has to make quick decisions and needs to have the makings of an assertive, but very communicative leader, ready to delegate and believe in team work. The director of photography is responsible for the general 'look' of the film and has the responsibility of filming a scene according to the director's wishes. S/he may also operate cameras, select lenses, and supervise lighting operations, technical maintenance and service.
The sound director is responsible for the film's sound requirements, from the design and planning pre-production phase through to recording and scheduling in production. S/he also manages the quality of the final mix in post-production.

b
Permission to shoot on certain locations
Availability of electricity on site
Availability of facilities on site
Technical issues
The need to contact a location agency

c
2 h   3 e   4 a   5 g   6 c
7 f   8 b   9 d

d
1 teams and equipment
2 health and safety
3 locations
5 shooting
5 lighting
6 extra lighting rigs; filters
7 most advanced
8 location agency

8a
Suggested answers
1 There are three different stages: pre-production, production, post-production (including distribution).
2 You could argue that they are all equally important.

b
1 A screenwriter has an idea for a film, which is pitched to potential investors.
2 A studio or a producer buys the rights to the film.
3 A producer, director, cast and camera/sound crew are hired to make the film.
4 The film is shot, and when completed is sent to the studio.

5 The studio signs a licensing agreement with a distribution company.
6 The studio or producer decides the number of prints of the film to make.
7 At screenings, the film is shown to potential buyers representing the cinema chains.
8 The buyers make an agreement with the distribution company about which films they wish to lease and fix the terms of the lease agreement (i.e. % of the box office).
9 Copies are sent to the cinemas a few days before they start showing the film.
10 When the film run ends, the film is returned to the distribution company, which pays the amount due.

c
2 studio   6 box office
3 licensing agreement   7 run
4 prints   8 screenings
5 lease

9c
1 Quite positive
2 The stars are an indication of how good the film is, based on the reviewer's opinion.
3 *Cert* = certified; this rating is used officially to refer to a film which is not considered suitable for children under the age of 15 to watch.

d
1 fact-based   4 voice-over
2 off camera   5 character
3 well-researched

e
1 But, Yet, Although
2 And
3 First of all, Secondly
4 So, Since

f
1 Although   4 secondly
2 But/Yet   5 Since
3 first of all   6 and

g
1 b   2 d   3 e   4 a   5 c

h
1 e   2 c   3 b   4 a   5 d

10a
1 Yes
2 It perhaps gives away too much, but then, as the review says, the film is fact-based, so most people who would go and see the film would already know the story.
3 Yes. He uses the words *best thing*, but this is not *too* over-emphatic.
4 Yes, for example: *successfully challenges the Chapman story*
5 Yes, for example: *… to explore, is the mysterious: Why?* or *The challenge for Piddington is to make the narcissistic nobody Chapman an interesting character.*

▇▇▇ Unit 6

1b
2 search function
3 sidebar
4 drop-down menu
5 hyperlink
6 shopping cart/basket

c
1 w-w-w-dot the Scottish Bookshop dot com
2 gavin underscore bennett at the scottish bookshop dot com

2a
The Scottish Bookshop's needs and objectives
Features of the website

b
2 T   3 F   4 F   5 T   6 T

c
Asking for definitions
Domain **what**, sorry? **What's** that?
What **exactly** are web hosting services?

Giving definitions
A web hosting service is a **type** of service which
…
A server is a **kind** of computer system which …

Bringing a meeting to a close
It's been really interesting **talking** to you.
I look forward to doing **business** with you.
Thanks for **coming** here today.

d
Asking for definitions
What do you mean when you say "…" ?

Giving definitions
Its function is …
It's used for …
It means …
You use it to …
It's like a …

Bringing a meeting to a close
I think we've covered everything.

e
1   so   3   If; 'll
2   the; the   4   Once; 'll

g
1   Yes
2   Comparatives
3   *Will*
4   *If* and *once* are followed by present tenses;
     in the main clause the subject is followed by
     will.
5   *After, as long as, as soon as, before, by the
     time, in case, unless, when, while*

h
1   Noun phrases
2   Book categories, bookshop information
3   A general welcome and the fact that more
     than one book can be bought at once
4   There are three lines per paragraph. To keep
     the amount of reading to a minimum, making
     the site quick and easy to navigate
5   *We* and *you*
6   To make the site quick and easy to navigate
     and also to make it seem more like an
     informal conversation than a formal written
     text.
7   Yes, there is a *Contact Us* link and a link to
     Gavin Bennett's email address.
8   Yes, it is clear, informative and simple to
     navigate.

3a
New media is any kind of media that can only be
created or used with the help of a computer.

b
Suggested answers
Old media: television, magazines, newspapers,
books, cinema, radio
New media: multimedia CD-ROMs, software,
websites, blogs, wikis, email and attachments,
interactive kiosks, interactive television, mobile
phones, podcasts, game consoles

c
Suggested answers
Broadband connection: websites, blogs, wikis,
email and attachments, interactive kiosks,
interactive television, game consoles
Free downloads: podcasts, websites, blogs,
mobile phones
High definition: interactive television, game
consoles
Video on demand: interactive television, mobile
phones, websites

4a
1 c   2 b

b
1   Premium satellite and digital television
     programming
2   To extend its customer base into Europe, to
     modify its payment system, and to be able to
     communicate directly with subscribers and
     non-subscribers
3   By establishing a content management
     application and setting up an interactive
     television application
4   Because they were difficult to build and
     delivered poor visual quality or had
     navigation problems
5   The content management application will
     manage the distribution of dubbed/translated
     content; the interactive television application
     will support multi-currency payment and
     social networking functions, and provide an
     exceptional user experience and high-quality
     presentation.
6   Television, video on demand, mobile phones,
     software, interactive television, computers,
     game consoles

c
2   At the time of writing, the world's biggest
     social networking websites are *MySpace* and
     Facebook.

d
1   F – this is a formal business document.
2   T
3   T
4   F – the statement uses *want* because it is
     much more direct.
5   T

e
1   adjectives
2   more
3   superlative

f
2   the latest   5   extensive
3   interactive   6   detailed
4   engaging

g
2   PVS   5   PVS
3   PVS   6   PVS
4   PS

h
Suggested answers
1   *Weather Wise* has a reputation as a leading
     provider of weather news.
2   *Weather Wise* wants to create an opportunity
     for its staff to find information easily.
3   The project will see the establishment of a
     collaborative portal.
4   Our solution will guarantee increased staff
     efficiency and faster management decisions.

5a
1   A blog is an online journal; the content is
     usually generated by a single person, who
     writes about topics that interest him/her.
     Blogs are a type of website, but not all
     websites contain blogs.

b
2   Information and articles about life in Spain,
     Spanish food and culture, and visiting Spain
     as a tourist

c
2 B   3 E   4 C   5 A

d
Block: definition 1
Post: definition 2

e
2 b   3 a   4 a   5 b   6 a
7 b

f
2   He uses the first person pronouns *I* and *we* a
     lot.
3   He uses interjections like *hey* and *wow*.
4   He uses dashes and exclamation marks.
5   He joins sentences with *and* rather than
     moreover, *however* and *therefore*.
6   He uses some slang words.
7   He usually uses contractions.
8   As a result of the above points, his style is
     informal.

g
2   useful   5   knowledgeable
3   titles   6   main
4   white space   7   mistakes

6b
Financial matters: processing payments, finding
an accountant who is willing to work with an
online business
Legal matters: privacy agreement, terms and
conditions agreement

d
1 So   2 Now   3 OK

e
1 T   2 F

f
Setting up the website: host company,
bandwidth, software, web design
Inspiration: books, websites

g
2   OK   5   Right; Er
3   Yeah   6   so wait
4   actually

h
2   yeah, OK   5   er
3   cos   6   so wait
4   actually   7   right, OK

i
to set up: a website, a business, a company
to draw up: an agreement, a contract, a
proposal, guidelines
to take on: a client
to outline: the main points, a proposal

Unit 7

1b

Raffaella Livingstone: general account manager
Cecily Valley: copywriter
Dave Terry: art director
John McEwans: brand manager
Frances Lohan: assistant brand manager
Headquarters: Milan (Italy)
Place of meeting: New York
Possible ad types: Print and TV
Next meeting: In ten days' time (1st August)

Target market and budget aren't mentioned.

c

Selling your company
2   many of
3   media
4   numerous
5   client
6   start

Expressing opinions and making comments
7   quality
8   excellent
9   impressive
10 effective

d

Suggested answers
2   numerous
3   computer, fashion, etc.
4   lots of, various
5   end-user, buyer
6   commence, kick off
7   calibre
8   superb
9   visually interesting
10 successful

f

2   be able to
3   'd say
4   longer; necessary
5   email
6   high standard; unforgettable
7   before you pay

2a

1   Raffaella Livingstone, general account manager at *Media Design Advertising*
2   John McEwans, brand manager at *The Daily Sunshine*
3   To summarise the details of the recent meeting

b

2   campaign   6   deadline
3   budget   7   adverts
4   print   8   reason
5   prime-time   9   queries

c

1   *Dear* plus name at the beginning and *Yours sincerely* at the end.
2   None
3   In the top left there is the recipient's / client's address and in the top right there is the sender's / company's address.
4   Underneath the recipient's address
5   Yes. However, it is written in note form and has section titles, which are two features that formal letters don't usually have.

3c

1   'You have to know' about the *New York Times*' advantageous subscription conditions and 'you have to know' what is happening around the world.
2   It is referring to the world. The message of the ad is that by subscribing to the *Intenational Herald Tribune*, which is easy to do, you will find it easier to make sense of our complex world.
3   Both adverts use direct statements ('Because you have to know', 'It's a complicated place') to grab the reader's attention and encourage him/her to read on. Both adverts also have hidden messages and include hardly any nouns.

4b

2   coach company / Greyhound USA
3   vermouth (drink) / Cinzano
4   tour operator / Thomas Cook
5   bank / Barclays
6   chocolate / Mars
7   magazine / TIME
8   beer / Miller

c

1   The Independent, Greyhound, Cinzano and Thomas Cook ads contain no nouns.
2   Verbs, adjectives and pronouns are used to convey the meaning instead.

d

2   repetition / 2/5
3   emphatic language / 3
4   word play / 7
5   personal pronouns / 1
6   rhyme / 4/6
7   metaphor / 8
8   comparisons / 2

e

Top 20 adjectives and verbs in advertising	
Adjectives	**Verbs**
1 new	make
2 good/better/best	get
3 free	give
4 fresh	have
5 delicious	see
6 full	buy
7 sure	come
8 clear	go
9 wonderful	know
10 special	keep
11 crisp	look
12 fine	need
13 big	love
14 great	use
15 real	feel
16 easy	like
17 bright	choose
18 extra	take
19 safe	start
20 rich	taste

f

2   Get (comparison, rhyme)
3   good, better (comparison)
4   new, new, new (alliteration / repetition)
5   best (comparison)
6   Take (personal pronouns)
7   big (personal pronouns)

5b

2   The main message that Mr McEwans, brand manager of *The Daily Sunshine*, wants to convey to his readers
3   The other important message that Mr McEwans wants to convey
4   A tree common in Madagascar, suggested as a symbol to represent freedom of speech and the sharing of ideas
5   Continent where baobabs can be found
6   Composer of the *New World Symphony*, the suggested soundtrack for the ad

c

The slogan uses word play: *lies* has a double meaning (*telling lies* and *lying* in the sun). The advert wants to stress the honesty and independence of the newspaper.

d

1   have you got   6   apart from
2   thoughts on   7   go for it
3   about   8   pursue
4   been done before   9   don't we
5   come up with   10   fantastic

e

Inviting people to express their ideas
What have you got?
Any thoughts on ... ?
What have you come up with?

Proposing ideas
How about ... ?
Why don't we ... ?

Accepting ideas
I think we should go for it.
If everyone agrees, let's pursue this idea.
That's a fantastic idea.

Rejecting ideas
Good idea, but I've got a feeling it's been done before, hasn't it?
Well, it seems like a good idea, apart from ...

f

Followed by a gerund (the *-ing* form):
how about, what about
Followed by infinitive without *to*:
we could, why don't we, let's

g

1   use   4   getting
2   doing   5   use
3   shoot

7a

2 a   3 g   4 b   5 e   6 d
7 f

b

2   Campaign aim
3   Voice-over
4   Super
5   Mood/Lighting
6   Shooting storyboard (SS)
7   Music
8   Timetable and logistics

8b

1   Four people

c

1 b   2 c   3 a

Unit 8

1b
Graph 1: bar chart
Graphs 2 and 3: pie charts

c
2 by
3 from
4 to
5 of
6 on

d
Sparkle's market share has decreased from 35.1% in 06/7 to 28% in 07/8.

2b
Talking about trends
Sales are falling.
There's been a dramatic 20% decline in the number of copies sold.
Sales have dropped from 151,056 copies to 120,845.
We lost 7 percentage points of our original market share altogether.
Our competitors' sales have risen by 5 percentage points and 2 percentage points respectively.

c
Phrases that describe positive change:
Profits are improving.

Phrases that describe negative change:
Sales are falling.
Our losses are increasing.
There's been a dramatic 20% decline in the number of copies sold.
Sales have dropped from …
We lost 7 percentage points of our original market share altogether.
Our competitors' sales have risen by …
Our profits slumped by 27%.

f
Implementing a new communication strategy
Online magazines

g
Restyling the magazine, bringing in a fashion consultant, running an advertising campaign, including new content.

3a
1 market segment
2 promotion
3 brand awareness
4 demand
5 trend report
6 communication strategy
7 needs; IMC
8 advertising campaign
9 readership; boost

b
2 a   3 f   4 g   5 d   6 b
7 e   8 c

4a
1 A public relations (PR) department is responsible for creating a favourable reputation of the company and its products/ services amongst the general public. A press office (PO) is responsible for answering questions from journalists about the company, its products and services and for providing them with information.
2 Events involving celebrities, the press, etc. can attract people's attention, or at least curiosity.
3 Celebrity endorsement can give potential customers confidence and create a sense of excitement around a brand or product.

b
1 The fact that budget has been approved for an advertising campaign.
2 Yes, they do.

c

Event	Event to relaunch *Sparkle*	Sep 5
Save-the-date	Send save-the-date for event	March
Photo shoot	Shoots with celebrities	Not fixed yet

d
1 will be for
2 have to
3 fix a date
4 important
5 planning
6 meantime
7 by

e
1 They are going to launch a browsable online version.
2 They will include an information sheet in the press kit.

f
2 save-the-date
3 press release
4 product placement
5 press kit
6 information sheet

5a
1 A press kit could contain background historical information on the company; an information sheet listing specific features, statistics or benefits of the product/service; details of past press coverage; photos; CD, DVD; software; video; sample products; etc.
2 A company might use a press kit for product launches, new company launches, mergers and acquisitions, news conferences, and other large promotional events and industry trade shows.
3 Public relations are a vital element in keeping contacts with the general public and taking care of the image of an organisation/ company. Organising events (for example, the launch of a new product) is one of their main responsibilities.

b
Having just a few more deadlines to meet
Proofs for the press kit
Sample designs for the cover
The hard work of everyone on the team
The difficulty in getting testimonials from celebrities
A slogan for invitation cards

c
That's good.
I'm sure you're doing an excellent job with the press kit.
Excellent!
Great job!
Well done to you and all of your team.
I'm really impressed with the way you've organised the event.
That's brilliant work.

d
1 The press manager says that she likes one particular photo showing a woman holding a rose, as it looks elegant and refined which is the kind of audience they are aiming to attract.

6a
1 A press release, or news release, is a public statement for the press to publish if they wish. It is intended to convince a reporter or an editor that a particular service, event, product or a person deserves to be in the news.
2 It can be part of a press kit (as, for example, in the *Sparkle* event); it can be sent alone or with a pitch letter.

b
1 Historical background
2 Innovative approach
3 Target market
4 Expert advice
5 Accessing the product

c
1 effective, powerful
2 short, focused
3 The writer is using adjectives to enhance his/ her description of *Sparkle*'s new features; the short, focused sentence structure helps the reader to maintain attention, and creates a greater impact than using long, complicated sentences.

7a
2 Advertising space is the major source of income for newspapers and magazines.

c
Effect on revenue from the sale of advertising space
Response of the press
Feedback from advertisers

d
1 T   2 F   3 F   4 F – 1.12   5 T

e
2 has been
3 've received
4 has been
5 've managed
6 received
7 has been
8 've seen
9 've regained

f
Most of the sentences in Exercise 7e refer to recent events that have an impact on the present, hence the use of the present perfect. Sentence 6, however, refers to a specific event in the past (receiving the report this morning) so uses the past simple.

g
1 Positive. The article seems to validate the communication strategy chosen by the team, particularly the use of celebrity endorsement and product placement. It is also complimentary about the new layout and design.
2 The magazine was launched in the mid-1970s, not in 1986. The online version of *Sparkle* should be available from October.

Acknowledgements

The authors and publishers acknowledge the following sources of copyright material and are grateful for the permissions granted. While every effort has been made, it has not always been possible to identify the sources of all the material used, or to trace all copyright holders. If any omissions are brought to our notice, we will be happy to include the appropriate acknowledgements on reprinting.

Text acknowledgements

Mirrorpix for the adapted article on p. 10 'Reclaim our streets: Hoodies and baddies' written by Vanessa Allen and Bob Roberts, Daily Mirror 13.5.2005. Copyright © Mirrorpix. Reproduced by permission of Mirror Syndication International; Solo Syndication for the adapted article on p. 10 'Under the hoodie is a child like yours' written by Suzanne Moore, Daily Mail 15.5.2005. Reproduced by permission of Solo Syndication Limited; Evening Star for adapted article on p. 16 'Thieves steal safe from kindergarten', Evening Star, 20 June 2007. Reproduced by permission of Evening Star, Ipswich; BBC Radio station logos and slogans on p. 18, reproduced by kind permission of BBC; Charlie Kaufman and Columbia Pictures for the extract from the screenplay 'Adaptation' on pp. 53-54. Copyright © 2002 Columbia Pictures Industries, Inc. All Rights Reserved. Courtesy of Columbia Pictures and Charlie Kaufman; Michael Wiese Productions for the adapted text on p. 56 'Filmmaking in the Digital Age' from www.mwp.com. Reproduced by permission of Michael Wiese Productions;

HowStuffWorks, Inc for the text on p. 60, courtesy of HowStuffWorks.com;

NI Syndication Limited for the adapted article on p. 61 'The Killing of John Lennon' written by Cosmo Landesman, The Sunday Times 9.12.2007. Copyright © NI Syndication Limited; Ben Curtis for the text on p. 70 'Notes from Spain – the story so far' from www.notesfromspain.com. Reproduced by kind permission of Ben Curtis; International Herald Tribune for the advertisement on p. 77 'It's a complicated place, but easy to subscribe to'. Copyright © 2008 the International Herald Tribune. All Rights Reserved; The New York Times for the advertisement on p. 77 'Because you have to know'. The New York Times. All rights reserved. Used by permission and protected by the Copyright Laws of the United States. The printing, copying, redistribution, or retransmission of the Material without express written permission is prohibited.

Photo acknowledgments

Alamy Ken Welsh p6, [apply pictures] p9, Janine Wiedel Photolibrary p10, Photos 12 p30 (Matt Damon image), Lourens Smak p63 (iTouch image), Danita Delimont p81 (r)
Archant Picture Desk p16
BBC p18 (logos)
Bigstockphoto.com Steve VanHorn p63 (BlackBerry)
Corbis Tom Grill p23, Kevin Dodge p39, William Whitehurst p45, Corbis Sygma p52 ('Get Shorty' image), C. Devan / zefa pp64, 71, Lester Lefkowitz p74, Sean Justice pp33, 84,
Sophie Clarke p17
Getty David Seed Photography / Taxi p18, Aaron Cobbett / Riser p30 ('Glorious' main cover image), Digital Vision p42, Heather Faulkner / AFP p48, Karl Lehmann / Lonely Planet Images p81 (l)
Haymarket Media Group p30 ('What Car?' image)
Herald Tribune p77 (r)
iStockphoto.com bubaone p60, John Woodcock p60, Dennis Cox p60, CostinT p63 (laptop)
Future Publishing p30 ('T3' and 'Simply Knitting' images)
Kobal Collection Columbia Pictures p52 ('Adaptation' image), Sweetland Films p52 ('Celebrity' image), Paramount p52 ('Sunset Boulevard' images)
New York Times p77 (left) **www.notesfromspain.com** pp69, 70

The National Magazine Company Ltd p30 ('Cosmopolitan' image)
Shutterstock Andi Hazelwood p18

Author's acknowledgements

The authors would especially like to express their gratitude to Clare Sheridan at Cambridge University Press for her guidance during the writing of this book. Thanks also to the Cambridge University Press editing team – Sara Bennett, Jeremy Day and to Nick Robinson – for their highly professional approach and patience.

The author Elizabeth Lee would like to thank Anna Meredith, Ben Curtis and Marina Diez, Adam Gilmore, Stephen Nicholls, and Francesco Fazio for sharing their help in all matters media. And above all she would like to thank Nan, Fabrizio, Joseph and Emily for their love and patience.

The author Nick Ceramella would like to thank such great media gurus as Ilaria D'Arco, David Eyre, Raffaella Di Vita, Flavia Muzi Falconi, Anastasia Kazakova, Silvana Pepe, Stefano Priori and Ivano Santovincenzo, for their time and advice. Thanks also to his 'better half', Marianna, who has tolerated, once again, with great forbearance, his shadowy presence, and has helped and encouraged him to accomplish this job.

Publisher's acknowledgements

Design and picture research: eMC design Ltd
Recording produced by: John Green and Tim Woolf

Cambridge English for … is a new series of ESP courses for different areas of English for Specific Purposes. Written for professionals by professionals, these short courses combine the best in ELT methodology with real professional practice.

Other titles in the series:

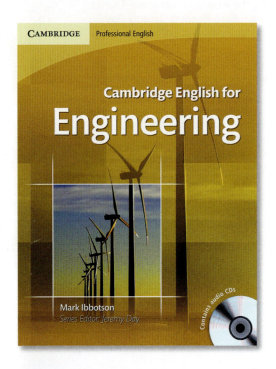

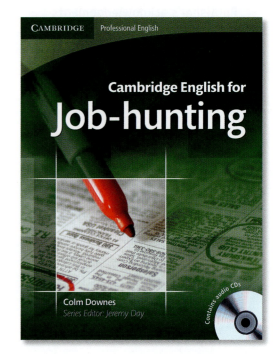

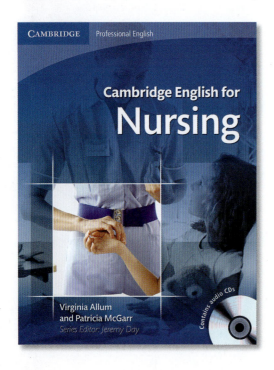